= VOLUME I =

THE HOLY EPISTLE TO THE
Hebrews

SERMONS ON A MESSIANIC JEWISH APPROACH

D. THOMAS LANCASTER

— VOLUME I —

THE HOLY EPISTLE TO THE
Hebrews

SERMONS ON A MESSIANIC JEWISH APPROACH

D. THOMAS LANCASTER

FIRST FRUITS OF
ZION

Copyright © 2024 D. Thomas Lancaster. All rights reserved.
Publication rights First Fruits of Zion, Inc.
Details: ffoz.org/copyright

Publisher grants permission to reference short quotations (less than 400 words) in reviews, magazines, newspapers, web sites, or other publications in accordance with the citation standards at ffoz.org/copyright. Requests for permission to reproduce more than 400 words can be made at ffoz.org/contact.

First Fruits of Zion is a 501(c)(3) registered nonprofit educational organization.

Printed in the United States of America

ISBN: 978-1-941534-69-4 : Hardcover
ISBN: 978-1-941534-93-9 : Softcover

Scriptural quotations are from The Holy Bible, English Standard Version, copyright © 2001 by Crossway Bibles, a division of Good News Publishers. Used by permission. All rights reserved.

Cover Art: Mykola G.

Quantity discounts are available on bulk purchases of this book for educational, fundraising, or event purposes. Special versions or book excerpts to fit specific needs are available from First Fruits of Zion. For more information, contact ffoz.org/contact.

First Fruits of Zion

Israel / United States

PO Box 649, Marshfield, Missouri 65706-0649 USA

Phone: (417) 468-2741
Website: ffoz.org

Comments and questions: ffoz.org/contact

About the Cover

Original watercolor painting depicting Herod's Temple.

To Maria Anne

To Our Children and Grandchildren

To Beth Immanuel Messianic Synagogue

CONTENTS

Introduction 1

Chapter 1: A Word of Exhortation 11
A proper introduction asks the same types of questions we ask of any piece of literature: what, when, who, to whom, and why.

Chapter 2: Solomon's Porch: The Historical Context 27
The first Jewish disciples of Jesus practiced Judaism as a Temple sect in Jerusalem, not Christians in danger of backsliding into Jewish practice.

Chapter 3: Sundry Times and Divers Manners
(Hebrews 1:1–2) 41
The apostles assigned the same weight to the words of Yeshua as to the words of the Torah and the Prophets.

Chapter 4: Radiance of Glory (Hebrews 1:1–3) 49
The Son of God is superior to the prophets and the angels because he is the manifestation of the Divine Wisdom and the image of God.

Chapter 5: Ten Testimonies (Hebrews 1:3–2:18) 61
A chain of ten linking proof texts demonstrates the Messiah's superiority over angels and establishes his authority.

Chapter Six: Spoken by Angels (Hebrews 2:1-8) 79

> If the Torah that came through angels demands respect, how much more so does the message that has come through the Messiah.

Chapter 7: The Perfect (Hebrews 2:6-18) 89

> The descent and ascent of the Son of Man in Psalm 8 alludes to the death of the Messiah, his resurrection, and ascension.

Chapter 8: The Family of God (Hebrews 3:1-6) 103

> The Messiah occupies the highest position of authority over the family of God, exalted even above the station of Moses.

Chapter 9: Enter My Rest (Hebrews 3:7-4:9) 111

> The story of the generation of Moses that perished in the wilderness provides a cautionary tale about the potential of forfeiting the kingdom and the World to Come.

Chapter 10: A Sabbath Rest Remains (Hebrews 4:9-13) 127

> The exhortation of Psalm 95 urges the generation to heed the Messiah, repent, and enter the ultimate Sabbath rest of the kingdom and the World to Come.

Chapter 11: The Messianic Psalm (Hebrews 4:14-16) 137

> The apostolic community interpreted Psalm 110 as a prophecy about the Messiah seated at the right hand of Glory.

Chapter 12: The Source of Eternal Salvation (Hebrews 5:1-10) . . 145

> The messianic prophecies of Psalms 2 and 110 indicate that Messiah has been named Son and high priest in the order of Melchizedek.

Chapter 13: Elementary Principles (Hebrews 5:11-6:3) 155

> Six elementary principles summarize the gospel message and constitute the milk of the Word of God.

Chapter 14: Things That Belong to Salvation (Hebrews 6:4–12) . . 167

> It's possible to fall away from Yeshua and forfeit the
> World to Come, but the one who endures to the end
> will be saved.

Chapter 15: Two Unchangeable Things (Hebrews 6:13–18) 179

> The disciple of Yeshua has confidence because God
> must keep the oath he made to Abraham and the oath
> he made to the Messiah.

Chapter 16: Melchizedek (Hebrews 7:1–17) 189

> Based on the criteria of a resurrected and
> indestructible life, the Messiah has entered the
> priesthood of Melchizedek.

Chapter 17: The Oath and the Law (Hebrews 7:18–28) 203

> The heavenly priesthood of the Messiah is efficacious
> for attaining eternal life without replacing the office or
> function of the Levitical priesthood.

INTRODUCTION

In the landscape of Bible exegesis, few epistles provide a greater challenge for a Messianic Jewish reading of the New Testament than the Epistle to the Hebrews. Its rich tapestry, woven with threads of deep Jewish tradition and messianic expectation, has been almost universally misunderstood as a sustained argument for Christianity's replacement of Judaism and the obsolescence of the Torah's Levitical worship system. The two volumes of this book contain a collection of sermons on the Epistle to the Hebrews that challenge this assumption by offering a post-supersessionist reading from a Messianic Jewish perspective on the text.

The Messianic Jewish Perspective

Messianic Judaism, as I know it, starts with the assumption that Christianity was originally Jewish. All the original members of the community of Jesus-followers were Jewish. Jesus, the apostles, and all the first disciples did not envision themselves as the authors of a new religion; they considered themselves to be a sect within greater Judaism—a reformation movement inspired by the teachings of Jesus (Yeshua) of Nazareth and by their conviction that he is the long-promised Messiah King. They did not hold Jesus or the gospel message in antithesis to the Law (Torah) of Moses. They upheld the words of Jesus:

> Do not think that I have come to abolish the Law or the Prophets; I have not come to abolish them but to fulfill them. For truly, I say to you, until heaven and earth pass away, not an iota, not a dot, will pass from the Law until all is accomplished. Therefore whoever relaxes one of the least of these commandments and teaches others to do the same will be

called least in the kingdom of heaven, but whoever does them and teaches them will be called great in the kingdom of heaven. (Matthew 5:17-19)

They practiced a religion that, in modern terms, can best be described as Messianic Judaism. Within a few decades, the charter members took a vote (Acts 15) to expand the membership to include non-Jews, but that did not, at first, alter the fundamentally Jewish nature of the institution.

Messianic Judaism can be understood as a branch of Judaism that honors Yeshua of Nazareth as Messiah and as the divine Son of God. The modern Messianic Jewish movement was born from Christian missionary efforts to evangelize Jews. In the late nineteenth century, Jewish believers in Jesus began to take ownership of their faith, eschewing Gentile Christian modes of worship and interpretation and working to establish an authentic Jewish expression of faith. In the 1960s and 1970s, the movement blossomed in the United States among young Jewish Christians of the Baby Boom generation. Since then, it has outgrown its original chrysalis as a Jewish missionary effort and has begun to emerge as an independent sect of Judaism, much as the communities of the original apostles did.

As was the case with those Apostolic-era Messianic communities, Messianic Judaism today includes a predominant number of Gentile participants. Many of those Gentile Christians have entered the movement seeking a more historically authentic form of Christianity. In that regard, Messianic Judaism is no longer an exclusively Jewish movement (if it ever was). Instead, it includes many "Messianic Gentiles" who, while not Jewish, nevertheless have found a spiritual home in the Messianic synagogue. I am one of those Gentiles, but I pastor a Messianic Jewish congregation, pray in a Messianic Jewish synagogue, and teach with the Messianic Jewish organization First Fruits of Zion. All this background information is necessary for the reader to understand the perspective from which I have written this book.

A Messianic Jewish Perspective on Hebrews

Here's my premise. The Epistle to the Hebrews exhorted Jewish believers to remain steadfast in their allegiance to Yeshua as the Messiah at a time when they were tempted to abandon their allegiance to him.

Why were they tempted to abandon their allegiance? Because the religious authorities threatened to banish them from the Temple and access to the priesthood. The Epistle to the Hebrews urges the original readers, "Don't let pressure from the Levitical authorities shake your faith in Yeshua. We have a high priest atoning for us in the heavenly Sanctuary."

The epistle presents a long and complex piece of Jewish exegesis to prove that the Levitical priesthood, the sacrifices, and the Temple in Jerusalem pertain only to this present world, which the writer says "is becoming obsolete and growing old [and] is ready to vanish away" (Hebrews 8:13). Yeshua said that the Torah and the covenant God made at Sinai will last until heaven and earth disappear, but according to the Epistle to the Hebrews, even heaven and earth are growing old, ready to disappear at the end of the age.

On the other hand, the priesthood of the Messiah atones for Israel in the heavenly venue. It functions under the auspices of the new covenant (issued in Jeremiah 31), which pertains to the Messianic Era and the everlasting World to Come. It's not about to disappear. Thus, the book of Hebrews argues, "Don't throw away the World to Come for the sake of this world. Don't throw out the heavenly high priest for the sake of approval from the earthly priesthood." While making this argument, the epistle carefully distinguishes between the Levitical priesthood and the priesthood of Messiah, between the Temple on earth and the heavenly Temple, between the Sinai covenant and the new covenant, and between this world and the World to Come. At no point does it substitute the Levitical priesthood with the heavenly, as replacement theology insists. Instead, it makes a distinction between the two, assigning them to their respective venues: this age and the age to come.

But if we read the Epistle to the Hebrews through the lens of replacement theology, inspired by a common misreading of Paul's epistles, it sounds as if it must be arguing for replacing the Levitical priesthood, replacing the sacrificial services, replacing the Temple on earth, and replacing the Sinai covenant. In this ill-conceived paradigm, Judaism is "becoming obsolete and growing old [and] ready to vanish away" because it is being replaced by a new religion that is not under the Law (Hebrews 8:13). Such a misinterpretation of the epistle fits hand-in-glove with the misinterpretation of Paul that has informed Christendom for most of two thousand years. This two-volume book of expository sermons augmented with commentary attempts to correct that misinterpretation.

Teaching through Hebrews Twice

I prepared and delivered this series of teachings to my community of faith, Beth Immanuel, a Messianic Jewish synagogue in Hudson, Wisconsin—twice. In January of 2003, only two months after the community of Beth Immanuel first launched, one of my new congregants approached me and asked me to teach a study on the book of Hebrews. I replied, "Yes, someday we might do that," meaning, "Within the next five years or so." The prospect of teaching through a long and difficult epistle sounded like a lot of work and not an ideal starting point for a new community. That same week, a second person asked me to explain the book of Hebrews from a Messianic Jewish perspective. I said, "You are the second person to ask me about that this week. Maybe we could do something on that subject—sometime." Later that same week, a third person approached me requesting a study on the book of Hebrews. I began to wonder if perhaps God might be trying to suggest something. At that point, the first person who had made the request contacted me again and repeated the request. The following Sunday night, after teaching an introduction to the book of Matthew at a local Lutheran Church, I asked, "Does anyone have any questions?" I assumed someone might ask something pertinent to the material we had been studying. One hand went up: "Explain the book of Hebrews." I can take a hint.

The following week, I began a series of expositions on the Epistle to the Hebrews. We taught through the book in eighteen weeks. The sessions were recorded. First Fruits of Zion reproduced the messages on audio CDs and distributed them under the title *Sichot on Hebrews*. In addition, I included a significant chunk of my exegesis on Hebrews 8–9 in a booklet titled *What About the Sacrifices?*, also published through First Fruits of Zion. The popularity of the audio series made me a little uncomfortable because I had not intended those teachings for broad distribution, and I had not done a thorough job with the material. Several of the lessons sounded sketchy at best. We continued to receive requests for the audios over the ensuing decade. *What About the Sacrifices?* became one of our most popular titles. In view of those successes, I decided to revisit the original material and expand on it. I delivered a new collection of forty-six sermons on the epistle for most of 2012, thus fulfilling what King Solomon said: "What has been will be again. There is nothing new under the sun."

The Conventional Route through Hebrews

As a collection of popular-level sermons originally presented to a congregation, it should go without saying that this is not an academic treatment of the epistle. Neither should it be considered an exhaustive commentary. It's simply a collection of sermons presenting a Messianic Jewish approach to reading Hebrews. I have intentionally attempted to keep it on a popular reading level (even if the ideas espoused will never be popular), free of footnotes and documentation. Nevertheless, I did attempt to engage with some of the broader scholarship touching on the epistle.

When initially preparing these sermons in 2003 and again in 2012, I compared several commentaries. I found them, for the most part, to be of little help in formulating a Messianic Jewish frame for interpretation. Instead, the commentaries I owned all followed the conventional Christian theological framework of traditional New Testament scholarship, which sees the Epistle to the Hebrews as a text emphasizing the superiority of Christ and the new covenant over and against the old covenant, including the Levitical priesthood and the sacrificial system. Unlike the Gospels, the Epistle to the Hebrews has not received the type of attention and critical rethinking that the teachings of Jesus received when scholars on the "Quest for the Historical Jesus" rediscovered his Jewish identity and context. Neither has the Epistle to the Hebrews received the type of reanalysis that Paul received when E.P. Sanders launched the "New Perspective on Paul," nor the recontextualization offered by post-supersessionist scholars who have argued for placing "Paul within Judaism." Hebrews has been left mostly untouched, making it the last bastion of replacement theology in the New Testament.

More recently, a slow trickle of progressive scholarship dealing with a Jewish approach to Hebrews has begun to appear. David Moffitt of the University of Saint Andrews has been doing most of the heavy lifting in this department. His two books on the subject, *Atonement and the Logic of Resurrection in the Epistle to the Hebrews* (Brill, 2011) and *Rethinking the Atonement* (Baker Academic, 2022), are indispensable. I have benefited from some correspondence with Moffitt while preparing for publication. In addition to Moffitt, I should point to Matthew Thiessen, who contributed an essay titled "Hebrews and the Jewish Law" to the T&T Clark anthology *So Great a Salvation* (2019). I was fortunate to obtain a copy of that book and his short, insightful essay before approving the final draft of this first volume of the commentary. I'm sure there are other scholars, somewhere out there, who would echo the conclusions of Moffitt and Thiessen, especially among those doing research toward a post-supersessionist reading of the New Testament. However, in January 2003, when I first began preparing for the series of teachings that would grow into this book, I had only a few academic-level Bible commentaries on hand, all of which followed the conventional route.

The conventional route leads us through the epistle to arrive quickly at the destination of replacement theology. That reading emphasizes the finality and superiority of the new covenant in Christ over the old covenant, including its priesthood and sacrifices. The epistle is explained as a theological argument for the transition from the old to the new. This traditional perspective on Hebrews and my own counterarguments can be summarized in the following points:

- CHRIST'S SUPERIORITY OVER ANGELS AND MOSES: Hebrews begins by asserting the superiority of Jesus Christ over angels and prophets, specifically Moses. Traditional interpretations hold that this demonstrates a new, elevated revelation in Christ, surpassing the messages delivered through angels and prophets in the Old Testament. In these sermons, I argue that the exaltation of the Messiah above Moses and the angels has its source in traditional Jewish interpretation of specific messianic texts and is intended not to supplant the Old Testament but to establish the Messiah's authority.
- THE NEW COVENANT: A central theme in conventional interpretations of Hebrews is the contrast between the old and new covenants. The new covenant, mediated by Jesus, is seen as replacing the old covenant, i.e., the Law (Torah) given at Mount Sinai. In these sermons, I argue that the new covenant presented in the prophecies of Jeremiah refers not to the cancellation

or replacement of the Torah or God's covenant with Israel in favor of a new religion but instead to Jewish eschatology's future hope of the Messianic Era and the World to Come.

- THE HIGH PRIESTHOOD OF JESUS: The epistle's depiction of Jesus as the heavenly high priest plays a key role in traditional Christian theology. This role is interpreted as surpassing the Levitical priesthood, with Christ serving as the perfect, eternal high priest, thereby replacing the Levitical priesthood ordained in the Torah. In these sermons, I argue that the messianic priesthood espoused by the epistle does not compete with the Levitical priesthood because it belongs to a different order of priests and operates in a different venue.

- THE OBSOLESCENCE OF THE OLD SACRIFICIAL SYSTEM: In traditional interpretations, the Epistle to the Hebrews depicts Christ as the perfect, eternal, once-for-all sacrifice for sin, unlike the repeated animal sacrifices of the Old Testament. His priesthood and sacrifice thereby render the old sacrificial system obsolete. The sacrifices under the old covenant are seen as mere shadows and types that find their true fulfillment in the sacrifice of Christ on the cross. In these sermons, I argue that the sacrifice of the Messiah corresponds to the Levitical sacrifices by way of analogy but does not function as a replacement for the Levitical sacrifices, accomplish the same purposes, or attain the same objectives. Neither did the death of Yeshua signal the cessation of the Levitical sacrifices. Instead, the Levitical sacrifices ceased a generation after the crucifixion with the destruction of the Temple in 70 CE.

- FAITH AND PERSEVERANCE: The epistle's exhortations to faith and perseverance are often read in light of the New Testament's broader message of salvation through faith in Christ, juxtaposed against a perceived reliance on the Law and works in the Old Testament. In these sermons, I argue that the epistle's exhortations to faith and perseverance should not be read through the lenses of Pauline arguments about works of the Law. That discussion is not in view whatsoever. Instead, the epistle exhorts its Jewish readers to observe the Torah without abandoning allegiance to Yeshua as the Messiah.

- WARNINGS AGAINST APOSTASY: The strong warnings against apostasy in Hebrews are ordinarily understood anachronistically as warnings against leaving the church. As such, they warn readers not to revert to Judaism. In these sermons, I argue that the Epistle to the Hebrews significantly predates the formation of a separate religion called Christianity; it was instead addressed to a Messianic Jewish readership who practiced Judaism as a natural expression of their faith in Yeshua. The warning against apostasy is not a warning against slipping back into Judaism (they never left Judaism) but an exhortation not to diminish or abandon allegiance to Yeshua as the Messiah.

It has now been twenty years since I first taught through Hebrews and ten years since I last visited the material. As I reopened the Microsoft Word documents containing my old sermon notes, I made numerous revisions for this book and filled in a lot of the gaps. I reorganized the original material and significantly expanded on it here and there to create a more thorough, sequential, verse-by-verse commentary. Nevertheless, the original ideas from that teaching series remain intact. If anyone is curious about how much revision I have done or how much my thinking has changed over the last decade, one can still hear the 2012 audio versions at bethimmanuel.org.

In addition, portions of the original sermons have found their way into various First Fruits of Zion publications, such as my Torah Club commentaries, the aforementioned *What About the Sacrifices?*, *What About the New Covenant?*, and *Elementary Principles*. The latter title consisted of a focused unit study on Hebrews 6:1–3, where the writer of the epistle complains about insufficient time to discuss "the elementary doctrine" of the Messiah. Unlike the author of the epistle, I had sufficient time, so I took up the challenge and developed those three verses into a series of twelve sermons, only the first of which is included in this current collection. (All twelve are still available through First Fruits of Zion under that title.) Moreover, this book follows in the footsteps of my previous commentaries, *The Holy Epistle to the Galatians* and *The Holy Epistle to Ephesians*, both of which came about as collections of Shabbat sermons on those epistles.

For the text of this book, I selected the English Standard Version of the Bible, but not without some hesitation. The reader will soon discover that I tend to quibble with the translators of that version over their rendering of the Greek text. Most of my attempts to correct the ESV occur when the translators have oversimplified a thought, misconstrued an idea, or completely missed a Jewish idiom, but in some cases, the argument is over translations colored by anachronistic theological suppositions. My arguments with the ESV clutter the commentary, but on a few occasions, I have amended the text directly. When that happens, I use square brackets [like this] to indicate my alterations.

Thank you to the good people at Beth Immanuel who encouraged me to teach on Hebrews in the first place. Thank you to my friend and colleague Boaz Michael of First Fruits of Zion, whose enthusiasm for the material inspired me to take it more seriously and to publish my thoughts. Thank you to my colleague Aaron Eby for valuable feedback on the teachings as I presented them week after week. Thank you to Dr. David Moffitt for important insights and for allowing me to bounce a few ideas off of him. Thanks goes to my father, Robert George Lancaster (of blessed memory), whose speculation about the *Sitz im Leben* of the epistle ultimately informed my thinking. Thank you to Steven Petersen for editing the original sermon notes. Thank you to all the *FFOZ Friends* who provide the financial support and spiritual encouragement necessary to make a book like this possible.

Whether you agree or disagree with the conclusions I set forth in these teachings, I believe that you will at least find some inspiration along the way in your own devotion to Yeshua and practice of the faith. May every disciple of our holy Master Yeshua who reads and studies the Epistle to the Hebrews receive an abundant blessing for life and for peace, both in this world and in the one to come.

Maranatha!

D. Thomas Lancaster
HUDSON, WISCONSIN
KISLEV 24, 5784

CHAPTER ONE:
A WORD OF EXHORTATION

A proper introduction asks the same types
of questions we ask of any piece of literature:
what, when, who, to whom, and why.

The Epistle to the Hebrews contrasts two mountains: Mount Sinai and Mount Zion.

First, we look back to remember Mount Sinai. It's a mountain that "may be touched, a blazing fire and darkness and gloom and a tempest and the sound of a trumpet and a voice whose words made the hearers beg that no further messages be spoken to them" (Hebrews 12:18-19).

Then we look forward to "Mount Zion and to the city of the living God, the heavenly Jerusalem," where "innumerable angels" gather in festival celebration along with "the assembly of the firstborn who are enrolled in heaven" (Hebrews 12:22-23).

The revelation at Sinai came through the fire on the mountain. Moses saw a burning bush that the fire did not consume. Through the flames of that holy fire, he received the revelation of God and encountered the Angel of the LORD. When he led the children of Israel to the mountain, the LORD descended upon it in flames of supernatural fire. From out of the fire, a voice spoke to the assembly of Israel:

> The LORD spoke to you out of the midst of the fire. You heard the sound of words but saw no form; there was only a voice. (Deuteronomy 4:12)

The giving of the Torah (the Law) at Mount Sinai was a grand debut, an unveiling of God unprecedented and unrepeated in human history, and it was utterly terrifying to those who were present. The people begged Moses to intercede and speak to them on God's behalf. They did not want to hear the terrifying voice that spoke from the fire on the mountain:

> We have heard his voice out of the midst of the fire ... This great fire will consume us. If we hear the voice of the LORD our God any more, we shall die. (Deuteronomy 5:24-25)

The book of Hebrews says that the voice from the fire "made the hearers beg that no further messages be spoken to them ... Indeed, so terrifying was the sight that Moses said, 'I tremble with fear'" (Hebrews 12:19-21).

Human beings had never before experienced a revelation of God of that caliber, nor have we since. Every person at the mountain heard the voice of the Almighty speaking audibly. For that brief duration of time, every one of them rose to a level of revelation higher than the loftiest prophets. But the apostles taught that the level of revelation obtained in the kingdom and the World to Come will exceed the experience at Mount Sinai. In the kingdom we will come before "God, the judge of all, and to the spirits of the righteous made perfect, and to [Yeshua], the mediator of a new covenant, and to the sprinkled blood that speaks a better word than the blood of Abel" (Hebrews 12:23-24).

Challenging the Conventional Interpretation

Conventional interpretations of Hebrews 12 set Mount Sinai and Mount Zion in antithesis. They are explained as types of the old and new covenants. Through the lenses of Christian supersessionism and replacement theology, the contrast in Hebrews 12 indicates that the new covenant supplants the old. It seems obvious enough. While speaking about the epiphany at Mount Sinai, the Epistle to the Hebrews says, "You haven't come to Mount Sinai; you've come to Mount Zion." In other words, "You haven't come to the Law; you've come to grace." Or, to put it another way, "You haven't come to the Old Testament, in which God was frightening and wrathful; you have come to the New Testament, the New Jerusalem, and God is much tamer now—full of love and grace." All these ideas are predicated on the common teaching that the old covenant—the covenant of the Law—was defective, but it has been replaced by a new, kinder, gentler covenant.

The majority interpretation of the book of Hebrews involves the following underlying assumptions:

- The book was written to Hellenist, Greek-speaking Christian Jews living in the Diaspora.
- The writer of the book of Hebrews wanted to warn Jewish Christians against returning to Judaism.
- The new covenant is superior to the old covenant.
- Christ's heavenly priesthood replaces the Levitical priesthood.
- Christ's death replaces the Levitical sacrificial system.
- The heavenly Temple replaces the earthly Temple in Jerusalem.
- Grace replaces the Law.
- Eternal life in Christ replaces the Sabbath.
- Obedience to the Law constitutes "dead works."

I believe that this replacement interpretation is anachronistic. It imposes later developments of church theology on a Jewish document, thereby misinterpreting it. If we can read Hebrews without the bias of replacement theology and Christian supersessionism, we may come much closer to the book's original message.

An Epistle to Messianic Jews

What do we know about the Epistle to the Hebrews? It is a short Greek document similar in tone and genre to the Apostolic-era epistles, yet distinct in certain ways from the other entries in the canon of the New Testament. The epistle has no superscription indicating the identity of the writer or his audience. It begins immediately with a lengthy discourse. It sounds thoroughly Jewish in its mode of argumentation and the type of propositions and symbolism it employs. Many churches, particularly in the West, were reluctant to sanction its use for public reading, which is to say that they were reluctant to grant it the status of what we now call canonical Scripture.

Is it a letter from the Apostle Paul? Several church fathers thought so. Clement of Alexandria claimed to have received a tradition that Paul wrote it in Hebrew and Luke translated it into Greek. Several early codices bundled it with Paul's letters, but Pauline authorship seemed unlikely for several reasons.

The Greek does not sound Pauline. The book presents a Greek style and rhetorical method more refined than Paul's writing. Neither does the theology resemble Paul's. It does not mention Gentile inclusion—the central theme in all of Paul's epistles. Lastly, in perhaps the most telling argument against Pauline authorship, the author of the epistle never talks about himself. Following the conventions of Greek writers and rhetoricians, Paul constantly inserts himself into his epistles. He makes heavy use of the singular pronouns "I," "me," and "my." These are virtually absent from the book of Hebrews. More often, the writer of Hebrews uses the plural pronouns "we," "our," and "us." The sequence of books in the New Testament canon reflects the uncertainty over the authorship of the Epistle to the Hebrews by placing it at the end of the Pauline epistles. Hebrews begins what some might refer to as the Jewish section of the New Testament. Unlike the Pauline epistles, Hebrews assumes an exclusively Jewish readership, as do the epistles that follow.

Light and Heavy

The book frequently employs a convention of rabbinic argumentation known as a *kol v'chomer*, meaning "from the light to the heavy." This argument takes the following form: "If something is true/not true for the light circumstance, how much more/less true is it for the weightier circumstance."

Rabbi Yeshua (Jesus) frequently used this Jewish hermeneutical principle. For example, he said, "If you then, who are evil, know how to give good gifts to your children, how much more will your Father who is in heaven give good things to those who ask him!" (Matthew 7:11). For this argument to be effective, the first thing—against which the second is compared—needs to be irrefutable. The two things being compared are not opposites; they do not stand in antithesis to one another. The power of the argument rests on the procession from the value of the first thing mentioned, in this example, "human fathers," to that of the greater thing, "the fatherhood of God." The fatherhood of God does not diminish the value of human fatherhood.

The author of Hebrews uses this form in Hebrews 12:

> See that you do not refuse him who is speaking. For if they did not escape when they refused him who warned them on earth, *much less will we escape* if we reject him who warns from heaven. (Hebrews 12:25)

Contrary to popular interpretation, this statement does not set the old covenant and the new covenant in opposition. The argument does not set Mount Sinai in antithesis to Mount Zion, the former being made obsolete while the latter supersedes it. Instead, the gist of the argument is this: "If you think that Moses is to be feared, who spoke to you on earth, *how much more* should you fear Yeshua, who speaks from heaven." The strength of the statement depends on the legitimacy and the continuing authority of Moses to magnify the revelation of Yeshua. In other words, "If the revelation through Moses at Sinai demands obedience, how much more does the revelation of Yeshua from Mount Zion." The revelation of Yeshua has greater weight; it is more fearsome, more awesome, more consequential, and brings more retribution for those who refuse him. This is not a "cheap grace" message that dispenses with the Torah; instead, it builds upon the foundation of the Torah.

The author concludes a few verses later with the words,

> Therefore let us be grateful for receiving a kingdom that cannot be shaken, and thus let us offer to God acceptable worship, with reverence and awe, for our God is a consuming fire. (Hebrews 12:28-29)

The fire that started at Mount Sinai continues to burn on Mount Zion. The latter does not replace the former.

A Proper Introduction

A proper introduction to the book of Hebrews requires us to ask the same types of questions we should ask about any piece of literature, particularly biblical literature: what, when, who, to whom, and why?

Answering these questions is a necessary step before we begin to formally study the epistle.

What?

What kind of document are we reading? The Bible contains many different literary genres, such as legal material, historical narratives, poetry, prophecy, wisdom literature, apocalypse, gospel, and correspondence (what we call "epistles").

When?

Knowing when something was written helps place the document in its historical context. Without historical context, we get lost quickly. For example, if you read a copy of the Gettysburg Address but assumed a U.S. president had delivered it in 1986, you would inevitably misinterpret its message.

Who?

If we know who the author is and already have some familiarity with his perspectives, experiences, and objectives, that knowledge will help us understand and interpret the author's intentions and message.

To whom?

The writer's audience helps establish an interpretative context. When reading someone else's mail, knowing the intended readership provides critical information. It also helps, when possible, to know where the recipient of a letter was located. Where was the document sent and where was it intended to be read?

Why?

If we can discover the occasion that inspired the author to take up pen and ink, we will have a key to interpreting the document's overall message. Every piece of biblical literature is "occasional," meaning that it was originally written for a specific purpose, to address a specific concern, or to resolve a conflict. With the possible exception of Moses, none of the Bible's writers sat down intending to write sacred canonical text. Every writer had a contemporary situation in view that he hoped to address.

Unfortunately, the absence of a superscription or accepted tradition makes answering the above questions regarding the book of Hebrews difficult. We are forced to do some detective work, engage in some speculation, and make educated guesses about authorship, date, and address.

What: A Word of Exhortation

What kind of document is the Epistle to the Hebrews? When the question is posed that way, it sounds as if the answer is obvious: it's an epistle. An epistle is a letter, a piece of correspondence or ancient mail sent from someone to someone. Obviously, the "Epistle to the Hebrews" must be an epistle. The problem with this answer is that the title "Epistle to the Hebrews" is merely traditional, perhaps a matter of inference, nominated by the early church. The book of Hebrews does not contain material typical of an epistle until the last chapter:

> Pray for us, for we are sure that we have a clear conscience, desiring to act honorably in all things. I urge you the more earnestly to do this in order that I may be restored to you the sooner. (Hebrews 13:18-19)

> I appeal to you, brothers, bear with my word of exhortation, for I have written to you briefly. You should know that our brother Timothy has been released, with whom I shall see you if he comes soon. Greet all your leaders and all the saints. Those who come from Italy send you greetings. Grace be with all of you. (Hebrews 13:22-25)

As with the subscriptions in the epistles of Paul, the book of Hebrews closes with a few personal notes, references to colleagues, and some greetings. This kind of language makes it obvious that we are reading a piece of correspondence sent from the author to a distant place, which makes it an epistle. But notice that our writer identifies the genre of the document otherwise. He says, "I appeal to you, brothers, bear with my *word of exhortation.*"

To exhort means "to incite by argument or advice, to make an urgent appeal." The English Standard Version uses the word "exhortation" to translate the Greek word *paraklesis*, which can also mean "encouragement." Notice how the English Standard Version translates the same word in Acts 13:

> On the Sabbath day they went into the synagogue and sat down. After the reading from the Law and the Prophets, the rulers of the synagogue sent a message to them, saying, "Brothers, if you have any word of encouragement [*paraklesis*] for the people, say it." (Acts 13:14–15)

In the days of the apostles, synagogues conducted daily prayer services meant to coincide with the times of the sacrifices in the Temple. On the Sabbath day, they augmented the prayer service with a public reading of Scripture and a word of *paraklesis*, a teaching. In addition to the prescribed liturgical prayers, the Sabbath synagogue service included three elements:

1. a reading from the Torah,
2. a complementary reading from the Prophets,
3. and a teaching that expounded on the two readings.

Paul's visit to the Galatian synagogue of Pisidian Antioch demonstrates the same three-part order of service:

1. "After the reading from the Law
2. and the Prophets
3. the rulers of the synagogue sent a message to them, saying, 'Brothers, if you have any word of encouragement [*paraklesis*] for the people, say it'" (Acts 13:15).

A passage in 1 Timothy may illustrate the same priority. In his first epistle to his disciple Timothy, the Apostle Paul gave instructions for conducting services in the local Messianic synagogue of Ephesus:

> Until I come, devote yourself to the public reading of Scripture, to exhortation, to teaching. (1 Timothy 4:13)

Similarly, in his epistle to the Romans, Paul mentions the role of "one who exhorts" within the community:

> Having gifts that differ according to the grace given to us, let us use them: if prophecy, in proportion to our faith; if service, in our serving; the one who teaches, in his teaching; *the one who exhorts, in his exhortation*; the one who contributes, in generosity; the one who leads, with zeal; the one who does acts of mercy, with cheerfulness. (Romans 12:6–8, emphasis added)

The author of the Epistle to the Hebrews can be described as "one who exhorts." Rather than relying on the cumbersome term "author of the Epistle to the Hebrews," the remainder of this study will use the term "the exhorter" to describe our otherwise anonymous author.

An Apostolic-era "word of exhortation" could be considered equivalent to the synagogal Hebrew term *d'rashah*, an exposition on a biblical text that might be offered in a first-century synagogue—in this case a first-century Messianic synagogue. This is a good description of the Epistle to the Hebrews. It reads more like rabbinic discourse than personal correspondence. It compares well with rabbinic literature such as the Midrash, a collection of teachings that the rabbis presented in the academies and synagogues.

The book of Hebrews is best understood, then, not as an epistle but as a first-century synagogue discourse, an early Messianic Jewish homily. It does contain epistolary salutations at the conclusion, but the author identifies the body of the document as a teaching. This teaching may have been delivered on a Sabbath and subsequently sent to other communities for their edification. Perhaps similar documents containing "words of exhortation," such as those found in the Epistle to the Hebrews, commonly circulated among the early believing communities and were distributed for public reading in the assemblies of Yeshua.

When: Before 70 CE

When was Hebrews written? When did the exhorter compose this teaching?

The earliest quotation from the book of Hebrews appears in Clement of Rome's *Epistle to the Corinthians*, also known as *I Clement*. Clement wrote his epistle around 95 CE, near the end of Emperor Domitian's life. That provides the terminus. We may assume that the Epistle to the Hebrews is earlier.

Internal evidence indicates that the Epistle to the Hebrews must have been written while the Temple still stood, that is to say, before 70 CE. Whenever the exhorter discussed the Temple, the priesthood, and the sacrifices, he did so in the present tense. For example, Hebrews 8:4–5 says, "There are priests who offer gifts according to the law. They serve a copy and shadow of the heavenly things."

Verb tenses in New Testament Greek are a continuing matter of academic debate, but in a simple reading, the present tense "they serve" seems to indicate that this book was written while the Temple still stood. I find indications that Hebrews was composed well before its destruction. The epistle does not refer to the first Jewish Revolt against Rome (66 to 73 CE), during which Rome destroyed the Holy Temple (70 CE)—remarks that we would expect to read if the epistle was written later, given that the discussion speaks extensively of the Temple ministry and its temporal limitations. If the exhorter knew about the Jewish war with Rome, he would have felt compelled to make some comment about it, but he did not. That omission pushes the date for the book back to the mid-sixties.

Moreover, the exhorter does not refer to the Neronian persecution in Rome (64 CE), another glaring omission in a book written to encourage believers to stand fast against persecution—especially when he explicitly references believers in Italy. If the document must predate that event, it may have been written as early as 62 or 63 CE. Setting the Epistle to the Hebrews in the early sixties will help us reconstruct the context that occasioned its writing.

Who: Someone Like Clement

Who was the exhorter? Who wrote the Epistle to the Hebrews? We know that the exhorter was not an apostle or one of our Master's original disciples. He makes that clear when he says in Hebrews 2:3, "[The message] was declared at first by the [Master], and it was attested to us by those who heard." This implies that the exhorter is a second-generation disciple who received the gospel from the apostles. He sounds like an apostle in that the exhortation has an air of authority, and the exhorter seems to transmit apostolic tradition. For example, he says, "In the days of his flesh, [Yeshua] offered up prayers and supplications, with loud cries and tears" (Hebrews 5:7). That sounds like an eyewitness report, something the exhorter could have obtained from one of the Master's original disciples, such as Simon Peter. Whoever he was, the exhorter speaks with an apostolic authority that we would not expect from a second-generation disciple unless he was of distinguished rank and well-recognized among the disciples of Yeshua.

As mentioned above, the absence of a superscription leaves the epistle anonymous and open to speculation. The early church badly wanted it to be an epistle of Paul. Some codices bundled it with Paul's letters, but the document is not Paul's style or language. The epistle is written in excellent Greek, unlike Paul's. As explained above, the theological concepts are not particularly Pauline. Moreover, Paul considered himself the apostle to the Gentiles, but the epistle to the Hebrews appears to have been written to Jewish disciples.

Nevertheless, it seems that the exhorter must have been someone within the Pauline entourage. He mentions Timothy having been released from imprisonment and waiting for his arrival. A close relationship with Timothy plausibly places the exhorter in Paul's company because Timothy was Paul's chief disciple.

The second-century church writer Origen addresses the authorship of Hebrews this way:

> But as for myself, if I were to state my own opinion, I should say that the thoughts are the apostle's [i.e., Paul's], but that the style and composition belong to one who called to mind the apostle's teachings and, as it were, made short notes of what his master said. If any church, therefore, holds this epistle as Paul's, let it be commended for this also. For not without reason have the men of old time handed it down as Paul's. But who really wrote the epistle, in truth, only God knows. (Origen, *Homilies on Hebrews*, quoted in Eusebius, *Ecclesiastical History* 6.14.1–4)

Some early church writers had the tradition that Paul's colleagues, Luke the doctor or Clement of Rome, might have been involved in the composition. Modern speculations include Barnabas, Apollos, and even Priscilla (see Acts 18:2–3), but that's pure speculation. We have no evidence or ancient report to support these theories.

Clement of Alexandria had a tradition that Paul's traveling companion Luke wrote the epistle, translating it from an Aramaic or Hebrew document originally composed by Paul:

> For as Paul had written to the Hebrews in his native tongue, some say that the evangelist Luke, others that this Clement himself, translated the epistle. (Eusebius, *Ecclesiastical History* 3.38:2)

This tradition is implausible. The Greek does not sound like Luke's, nor does it betray any hint of having been translated from a Semitic original. Eusebius, the fourth-century bishop of Caesarea, cites Clement of Alexandria's Lukan-Pauline theory. However, he favors an alternative tradition that suggests that Clement of Rome might have been involved in the composition. An early tradition about Clement of Rome indicates he was a Roman disciple and convert to Judaism who followed Peter but also had contact with Paul. Paul referred to him as one of his fellow workers, if indeed this is the same Clement (see Philippians 4:3). According to tradition, Clement served as Peter's chief disciple, as Timothy did for Paul and as Peter did for the Master. Bishop Eusebius cites a tradition identifying Clement as the exhorter:

> Others claim that it was Clement himself. This seems more probable because the epistle of Clement and that to the Hebrews have a similar character in regard to style, and still further because the thoughts contained in the two works are not very different. (Eusebius, *Ecclesiastical History* 3.38:2-3)

The consensus of modern scholarship disagrees with this assessment. Although the style of Clement's epistle sounds similar and at points identical to that of the book of Hebrews, most critics dismiss the similarities by suggesting that Clement intentionally imitated the style of the epistle to the Hebrews. They object to Clementine authorship primarily on the basis that the theology of the epistle runs counter to that espoused in *1 Clement*. Whereas the book of Hebrews appears to teach the cancellation of the Temple and the sacrificial system, *1 Clement* seems to regard that system as a worthy model for churches to emulate with respect to ecclesiastical authority. Moreover, Clement of Rome endorses the ongoing authority of the Torah and the Levitical rules, whereas the book of Hebrews is understood to supplant those things. On this basis, scholars object that the same writer could not have written both *1 Clement* and the Epistle to the Hebrews.

However, when we read the Epistle to the Hebrews from a post-supersessionist perspective, that objection vanishes. Hebrews does not need to be interpreted as teaching the cancellation of the Temple and the Levitical system. On the contrary, it can be read to completely endorse the Levitical system in the same manner that Clement does. If we adopt a post-supersessionist perspective on the book, Clement of Rome need no longer be disqualified as a likely candidate. His authorship enjoys the support of a strong historical tradition and a similarity of thought and style. It's beyond the scope of this book to consider that theory further, but even if the exhorter was not Clement of Rome, he must have been someone very much like him—a second-generation disciple who spoke with nearly apostolic authority, moved in the Pauline circle, and knew believers from Italy: "Those who come from Italy send you greetings" (Hebrews 13:24).

To Whom: Greek-Speaking Messianic Jews

To whom was the Epistle to the Hebrews written? It was written to Jewish followers of the Master. The content of the epistle makes that much clear. Unlike the epistles of Paul, Hebrews seems to address Jewish disciples directly. It scarcely mentions Gentiles. It presumes a readership with sophisticated biblical literacy and familiarity with midrashic and rabbinic argumentation. We have already suggested that Hebrews is best understood as a word of exhortation to a Messianic Jewish assembly or synagogue.

The intended readers were Greek-speaking Jews. They were probably not Aramaic-speaking Galileans like the family of the Master from Nazareth or the disciples from Capernaum. They were more likely Hellenist Jewish believers like Stephen and Philip the deacon. Many scholars suggest that the epistle might have been written to a community of Greek-speaking Jewish believers in the city of Rome because Hebrews 13:24 says, "Those who come from Italy send you greetings." However, that greeting provides thin evidence for a Roman address. The Greek could also be read, "Those of Italy send you greetings," suggesting that it was written *from* Rome, not *to* Rome. Several internal clues suggest that the letter was intended for Jews in Judea rather than for Jews in Rome. The discussion about the Temple, priesthood, and sacrifices would have had meager relevance to a community of Roman Jews because they had no access to those privileges in the first place. Most of them would never have visited the Temple in Jerusalem. Consider the concern over sacrificial foods expressed in this verse:

> It is good for the heart to be strengthened by grace, not by foods, which have not benefited those devoted to them. We have an altar from which those who serve the tent have no right to eat. (Hebrews 13:9–10)

The concern here involves sacrificial foods, sacrificial meat, and bread obtained from the Temple and the Levitical priesthood in Jerusalem (Cf. 1 Corinthians 9:13, 10:18). The discussion would have been relevant only to those disciples of Yeshua who had been accustomed to eating the sacred portions. Those sacred foods could not be obtained anywhere but Jerusalem, nor could they be eaten anywhere but Jerusalem. The statement would make the most sense if the epistle were written to a Judean community of Greek-speaking Jews living in the environs of the holy city. This premise finds further support in the discussion of "the city":

> [Yeshua] also suffered outside the gate in order to sanctify the people through his own blood. Therefore let us go to him outside the camp and bear the reproach he endured. For here we have no lasting city, but we seek the city that is to come. (Hebrews 13:12–14)

Was there a community of Greek-speaking Jewish disciples in or around Jerusalem? According to the book of Acts, the Greek-speaking community of Jewish disciples in Jerusalem was so large that the apostles had to appoint seven Greek-speaking deacons to manage it. Many of the Greek-speaking Jews in Jerusalem attended the synagogue of the Freedmen, which catered to Jews from Greek-speaking provinces (see Acts 6:1–6, 9).

For this study, we will consider the possibility that the exhorter addressed his word of exhortation to Jewish disciples of Yeshua accustomed to access to the Jerusalem Temple. They might have been Greek-speaking disciples in Rome or elsewhere in the Diaspora who ordinarily made regular pilgrimages to the Temple in Jerusalem. They might have been the Greek-speaking community of Jewish disciples in Judea. In either case, we know the epistle was written to Greek-speaking Jewish believers who formed some type of assembly or Messianic synagogue somewhere in the first-century Roman world, and we can infer that this assembly of Jewish disciples was concerned about access to the Temple in Jerusalem and to its services.

Why: Exclusion from the Temple

What occasion inspired the book of Hebrews? The exhorter made several statements that reveal the intention behind the epistle: "Let us hold fast our confidence"; "let us hold fast our confession"; "hold fast to the hope set before us"; "let us hold fast the confession of our hope without wavering." He says, "Do not harden your hearts"; "do not throw away your confidence"; "do not neglect assembling together"; "do not refuse him who is speaking"; "do not be led astray; do not be deceived." Obviously, the epistle addresses a potential apostasy. (The word "apostasy" means "falling away.") The exhorter intended to warn the Jewish disciples of Yeshua about the dangers of forsaking the path of discipleship. Some external or internal pressure had made apostasy from Yeshua faith a likely possibility. The arguments presented in the word of exhortation attempted to correct that situation by presenting the incomparable splendor of the priesthood of Messiah and its efficacy for securing eternal life. The word of exhortation urged and encouraged Jewish believers to remain steadfast in their commitment to Yeshua of Nazareth.

This word of exhortation remains relevant to disciples today. In the modern era we face a growing inclination toward apostasy among the disciples of Yeshua, that is, a tendency to fall away from the Master. The allure of secularism continues to draw people of faith like a magnet. Once-devout disciples easily slip into the post-Christian values of the modern culture, absorbed by the spirit of agnosticism and narcissistic hedonism. For us, the exhortation in the book of Hebrews can serve as a warning against modern secularism—the spirit of the age.

CHAPTER TWO:
SOLOMON'S PORCH: THE HISTORICAL CONTEXT

> The first Jewish disciples of Jesus practiced Judaism as a Temple sect in Jerusalem, not Christians in danger of backsliding into Jewish practice.

Where did the first Christians go to church? Did they build a church in Jerusalem? When did they install the first steeple? These questions are anachronistic. The first disciples were not Christians as we understand the term "Christian" today; they were Jews who practiced Judaism. That is to say, they did not practice what we would recognize as Christianity because Christianity did not yet exist as a religious entity outside of the broader tent of Judaism. They did not attend a church but instead went to the synagogue.

They did have a common place of assembly where the Jewish Yeshua believers in Jerusalem gathered every day for prayer, worship, and teaching: They gathered on the Temple Mount, a place called Solomon's Colonnade, sometimes translated as Solomon's Portico or Solomon's Porch.

The colonnaded courtyard consisted of a portico of monolithic white-marble pillars roofed with cedar beams. The portico ran along the eastern wall of the Temple Mount opposite the Mount of Olives. When the Hasmoneans and Herod the Great expanded the Temple Mount, the Kidron Valley on the east prevented expansion of the Temple court in that direction, so the colonnade that faced the Mount of Olives marked the line of the original Temple Mount from the time of King Solomon. That is why the people called the eastern portico Solomon's Colonnade.

Solomon's Colonnade stood above an original section of retaining wall on the Temple Mount. Josephus described it:

> These colonnades belonged to the outer court, and were situated above a deep valley, and had walls that extended four hundred cubits, built of square, white stones. The length of each stone was twenty cubits, and the height was six cubits. This was the work of King Solomon. (*Antiquities of the Jews*, 20:9.30)

The apostolic community expected the returning Messiah to enter the Temple from the east, and they wanted to be the first to greet him. The great eastern gate, the main entrance of the Temple, opened into that colonnade. Today's sealed eastern gate, popularly known as "the Golden Gate," probably preserves the location of the Second Temple's eastern gate.

The Prophet Zechariah predicted that the Messiah would arrive on the Mount of Olives and then enter the Temple through the eastern gate. Ezekiel saw a vision of the Divine Presence of God returning to the Temple through that same gate. When Muslims walled up the two portals of the eastern gate in the ninth century, Christians took note of the prophecy in Ezekiel:

> This gate shall be shut; it shall not be opened, and no one shall enter by it, for the LORD God of Israel has entered by it; therefore it shall be shut. (Ezekiel 44:2 NASB)

After the outpouring of the Holy Spirit in Acts 2 (which most likely occurred in the colonnade), the disciples used Solomon's Colonnade as their regular place of assembly (Acts 3:11, 5:12). This porch served as the meeting place of the first church, so to speak.

A New Insight

In the mid-1990s, my father and mother visited my family at our home in Saint Paul, Minnesota. Of course, they mainly came to visit the grandbabies—at that time, we had three little boys. During the visit, my father spoke to me about the historical context of the book of Hebrews. He was a pastor, and he had been recently studying the Epistle to the Hebrews on his own; perhaps he was teaching on it at the time. He shared a few of his observations with me.

He thought it strange that the exhorter said in Hebrews 13:22, "I have written to you briefly." Briefly? This comment puzzled my father. In fact, Hebrews is one of the longer epistles. My father suggested that initially, the book of Hebrews might have been considered two separate documents: a long one that consisted of the main teaching of the epistle and a short letter attached to the longer document that begins near the end of chapter 13. My own studies in the epistle support that theory. As explained in the previous chapter, most of the text is not really an epistle but a "word of exhortation" originally intended to be delivered to a first-century Messianic Jewish assembly. Only the closing remarks in chapter 13 can be considered epistolary.

In the same conversation, my father speculated about the occasion that might have inspired the writing of the Epistle to the Hebrews. As he mused over the question, mulling it over, he said, "I think those Jewish Christians had been kicked out of the Temple, and they were at a real loss and did not know what to do about it." I have to credit my father with this suggestion because I don't think it would have occurred to most pastors. Most pastors and Christian Bible teachers assume that the early Jewish Christians forsook the Temple, the priesthood, the Levitical system, and certainly the animal sacrifices from the outset, or from the day of the resurrection of Jesus or at least the day of Pentecost. You can't get kicked out of some place you don't attend.

This assumption is so much a part of the contemporary theological paradigm that it often goes unchallenged. Didn't Jesus teach against the Temple all the time? Didn't he say, "Neither on this mountain nor in Jerusalem will you worship the Father ... The true worshipers will worship the Father in spirit and truth" (John 4:21–23)? Didn't he predict the destruction of the Temple? Didn't his death replace the animal sacrifices?

From that supersessionist perspective, the epistle is about the danger of a Christian Jew falling back into Judaism. But consider my father's suggestion. What if the book of Hebrews wasn't a warning against backsliding into Judaism and the Temple? What if the author penned it as a consolation to a confused and shaken community that had recently been forcefully ejected from the Temple and now suffered under pressure to renounce the name of the Master?

In the course of these studies, we will test my father's suggestion against the contents of the epistle. His interpretation has several advantages. It does not anachronistically imagine the development of an independent Christian identity outside Judaism. It does not require Jesus to abolish the Torah or the Levitical system. It explains the arguments within the epistle, and it fits with what we know about the early believers and their relationship to the Temple.

The Apostles and the Temple

Yeshua's disciples revered the Temple because their Master revered it. He regarded the Temple as his "Father's house." As a boy, Yeshua had been reluctant to leave the Temple courts. As an adult, he could be found in the Temple teaching and attending the festival services. He spent the last days of his life in the Temple. In sorrow and tears he predicted its coming destruction. He drove the moneychangers from its courts while quoting the Prophet Isaiah, declaring, "It is written, 'My house shall be called a house of prayer'" (Matthew 21:13). He was zealous for the Temple; "his disciples remembered that it was written, 'Zeal for your house will consume me'" (John 2:17). He promised to return to the Temple when Jerusalem welcomes him with the words, "Blessed is he who comes in the name of the Lord!" (Luke 13:35).

The last verse of the Gospel of Luke tells us that after the Master's ascension, his disciples "were continually in the temple blessing God" (Luke 24:53). They were probably in the Temple, perhaps even in Solomon's Portico, when the Holy Spirit was poured out upon them on the day of Pentecost. Is it any wonder that the Temple became the locus of the apostolic community?

The book of Acts says that they devoted themselves to the prayers that coincided with the daily times of sacrifice in the Temple (Acts 2:42, 3:1). They were "day by day, attending the temple together" (Acts 2:46). Acts 5 tells us that every day the believers "were all together in Solomon's Portico" and that "the people held them in high esteem" (Acts 5:12–13). Even when the Sanhedrin ordered them not to speak in the Temple, they persisted. An angel of the LORD instructed them, "Go and stand in the temple and speak to the people all the words of this Life" (Acts 5:20).

Like Anna the prophetess, of whom it says, "She did not depart from the temple, worshiping with fasting and prayer night and day" (Luke 2:37), the first Jewish believers were "day by day, attending the temple" (Acts 2:46). They continued to assemble there in the name of Yeshua (Acts 5:42). Perhaps because of their constant presence, "a great many of the priests became obedient to the faith" (Acts 6:7). What did these priests do when they became disciples? Did they quit the priesthood? Did they say, "Sorry, I can no longer serve as a priest because Yeshua is the only true sacrifice?" On the contrary, they continued to minister according to the commandment and their holy obligation, but they did so with new enthusiasm. For years they had splashed the blood against the altar without understanding any messianic or redemptive significance, but now they did so with spiritual insight and conviction, seeing in those services the shadow cast by the suffering of the Son of God himself. In light of their new perspectives, they could now see the Temple rituals as tokens of the glorious hope of the redemption of Israel and all mankind.

The Temple Sect

We are commonly taught that Christ hated the Temple and that the early Jewish believers eschewed the Temple. The biblical narratives indicate otherwise.

Stephen was arrested and charged with speaking against the Temple in the name of Yeshua. The book of Acts states unequivocally that the charges brought against Stephen for speaking against the Temple and the Torah were false allegations raised by enemies of the Master (Acts 6:13-14). Stephen denied the charges.

The Jewish believers in Jerusalem did not build a church or even a synagogue; their locus was the Temple. Even the name of their sect, "the *ekklesia*," may have originated from Temple terminology. *Ekklesia* (assembly) is the Greek word translated as "church" in our Bibles, but in the Hebrew Scriptures its equivalent, *kahal*, typically refers to an assembly in the Temple. This nomenclature may have evolved quite naturally. If the early Jerusalem believers were every day assembling in the Temple as the book of Acts indicates, one can imagine a natural evolution in which the believers began to refer to themselves as "the assembly."

To facilitate daily access to "the assembly" in the Temple, the believers in Jerusalem practiced a type of communal living, selling their possessions and holding everything in common as they lived in Jerusalem. (Perhaps Paul's congregations did not follow that model of corporate ownership because his communities were in the Diaspora, far away from the Temple in Jerusalem.) Simon Peter did not want to go back and live in Capernaum. James and John, the sons of Zebedee, did not want to go back to live in Bethsaida. James, the brother of Yeshua, did not want to go back to Nazareth to live. Nathanael did not want to go back to Cana. Many disciples from distant locations relocated to Jerusalem. The Greek-speaking Jews from the Diaspora wanted to remain in Jerusalem as well, near the Temple, near the apostles, and near the Father's House. For example, Joseph Barnabas sold his property in Cyprus and moved to Jerusalem. The Temple drew the apostolic community together.

As we move forward in the history of the early believers, we meet the Apostle Paul, who, after his encounter with the Messiah, eventually returned from Damascus to Jerusalem. Where did he go when he arrived in the holy city? Directly to the Temple. In the Temple he experienced a revelation of our Master Yeshua. To that same Temple he continued to return as often as possible until, eventually, Roman soldiers carried him out of the Temple.

Apostolic Sacrifices

Not only did the believers congregate in the Temple and participate in the prayer services at the times of sacrifice, but they also continued to bring sacrifices. This much is obvious. If they had not continued to participate in the sacrifices, the New Testament surely would have recorded that deviation from standard Jewish practice, but it does not. If they had turned their backs on the Levitical system, the New Testament writers would have mentioned that detail because it would have marked a radical departure from normative Judaism.

Instead, the book of Acts notes that they continued to participate in the routine sacrificial services. Nearly thirty years after the death and resurrection of the Messiah, Paul "went up to worship in Jerusalem" (Acts 24:11) to keep the Festival of Pentecost and "to present offerings" (Acts 24:17). He joined four other believers who, like himself, had undergone nazirite vows. The five of them needed to offer a series of animal sacrifices to complete their vows (Acts 21:23-26). Paul agreed to pay for the expenses of the other Nazirites, meaning he personally financed the sacrifice of ten lambs and five rams (Numbers 6:13-21). The narrative of the book of Acts relates the story of these sacrifices matter-of-factly as if believers offering sacrifices in the Temple were nothing unusual. More importantly, James and the elders of the apostolic community pointed to Paul's participation in sacrificial Levitical rites as evidence to other Jewish believers that he was still living "in observance of the law" (Acts 21:24) and therefore kosher, despite what he might be teaching Gentiles about their level of obligation to the Torah.

Paul defended himself before Festus, saying that he only "went up to worship in Jerusalem" (Acts 24:11). In a Jewish context, to "worship in Jerusalem" means to offer sacrifice and prayer at the Temple as prescribed by God in the Torah. Paul went on to say, "After several years I came to bring alms to my nation and to present offerings" (Acts 24:17). The Greek word translated as "offerings" (*prosphoras*) means "sacrifices." Paul declared that he went to Jerusalem to present sacrifices.

James, the first bishop of Jerusalem, second only to Yeshua himself, constantly remained in the Temple on his knees in prayer:

> [James] used to enter the Sanctuary alone, and was often found on his knees beseeching forgiveness for the people, so that his knees grew hard like a camel's from continually bending them in worship of God and beseeching forgiveness for the people. Because of his unsurpassable righteousness he was called "The Righteous One," and Oblias, "Bulwark of the People, and Righteousness." (Eusebius, *Ecclesiastical History*, 2:23:7, citing Hegesippus)

The predominant supersessionist theology regarding the sacrificial system maintains that the death of Jesus served as the final sacrifice and that his death abolished the sacrificial system. The biblical evidence indicates that the early apostolic authorities did not share this interpretation.

If the death and resurrection of the Messiah had canceled the Levitical worship system, why did the apostolic community still engage in it? Why did Paul bring sacrifices? Why did the apostles continue to assemble in the Temple? Why did James spend his hours there in prayer?

New Perspectives

We have just seen a snapshot of the earliest disciples of Yeshua right out of the Bible: scrupulously Torah-observant Jews, devoted to the Temple and its services, faithfully serving the Master. That we need to spend a whole chapter trying to establish the continuing validity of the Temple in the lives of the first-century believers indicates how far our theology has drifted from that of the early believers, from Paul and James and Steven and Peter, and even from the writer of Hebrews.

The Jewish disciples in the first century could be described as a Temple sect. The appellation applies not just to the church in Jerusalem and Judea but to Jewish believers everywhere. The mother congregation in Jerusalem had planted all the assemblies of Yeshua throughout Judea, Samaria, Galilee, and the Diaspora. They looked to the Jerusalem assembly and emulated her. They submitted to the authority of James and the apostles in Jerusalem. Jewish believers from Diaspora congregations, whether from Alexandria, Antioch, Rome, or any place in between, came to Jerusalem for pilgrimage festivals. Acts 2 gives a list of the places from which Jews traveled to attend the festivals. They came from all over the world. (In that regard it does not matter whether the Epistle to the Hebrews was originally addressed to believers in Jerusalem or Rome; all Jews considered the Temple to be the geographical center of their faith.)

You will probably not hear these ideas taught outside Messianic Judaism. Supersessionism comes with a heavy anti-Temple bias. That bias is only one facet of the broader anti-Torah and anti-Jewish conceit that underlies all of replacement theology. Supersessionism assumes that Christ has replaced the Temple's sacrifices, the church has replaced the Temple, grace has replaced the Torah, and Christians have replaced the Jewish people. When we think of Yeshua's Jewish disciples as anti-Temple and anti-Torah, we inevitably misunderstand the New Testament. It's like trying to understand the religion of the pope while insisting he isn't part of the Roman Catholic confession. It's backward.

The Torah mandates the sacrificial system for Israel, and the Torah says the laws of sacrifice are eternal statutes. Either the Torah is correct, or it's wrong, and if it's wrong, the Bible is out of business.

Plots and Schemes

In the previous chapter, I suggested that the book of Hebrews seems to have been written prior to the fall of the Temple, prior to the beginning of the Jewish Revolt, and even prior to the beginning of the Neronian persecution, placing its writing in the early sixties of the first century.

In the early sixties, the relationship between the Jewish believers and their archenemies, the Sadducees, further deteriorated. The Sadducees denied the resurrection. They were the ones responsible for most of the early persecutions against the disciples. They were always at odds with the disciples of Yeshua. Around 62 CE, a Sadducean priest named Chananyah ben Chananyah rose to power. He was the son of Chananyah ben Seth, who is called Annas in the Gospels. Thirty-two years earlier, Chananyah ben Seth had conspired with his son-in-law Caiaphas and the Roman procurator Pontius Pilate to put Yeshua to death.

In 62 CE, the Roman procurator of Judea, Festus (whom we meet in Acts 24), died unexpectedly. Before Rome could replace him, Chananyah ben Chananyah convened an illegal Sanhedrin of Sadducees. They arrested James, the brother of the Master, and several other prominent believers. James received a death sentence. They placed him at the pinnacle of the Temple overlooking the Kidron Valley. They demanded a public renunciation of his faith in Yeshua. James refused. They threw him down. Miraculously, he survived the fall. They stoned him, and finally, a blow to the head with a fuller's club ended his life. The death of James was not just another martyrdom. James had presided over the entire believing community as the *nasi*, the steward of the throne of David, the head elder and bishop of bishops. He was Yeshua's own brother—flesh and blood. His death was a grievous blow to the community.

The chief priests among the Sadducees then conceived a plan that might have been intended to intentionally dislodge the community of believers from their accustomed place of worship. They approached King Agrippa (II) with a building request. They pointed out that the laborers working on the massive Temple remodeling project, first instituted by Herod the Great, had finally completed their task. The conclusion of the project left eighteen thousand laborers unemployed. The chief priest suggested a new phase to the project that would involve remodeling Solomon's Colonnade from the valley floor up.

The Sadducean priests helpfully volunteered to finance the project with excess money from the Temple treasury. Of course, the remodeling project had the added benefit of forcing the believers out of their customary gathering place.

King Agrippa vetoed the plan. He objected, "It is easy to demolish a building, but not so easy to build it up again." He uttered those words just a year or so before the Jewish Revolt began. In retrospect, his words sound prophetic, and they can be compared with the Master's saying, "Destroy this temple, and in three days I will raise it up" (John 2:19).

The Ban

I did not yet know any of this history about the early believers that day when my father was discussing the book of Hebrews in my living room, and neither did he. It has taken me years to piece the story together bit by bit. But now we come to the speculative part of the story my father suggested as the key to interpreting the Epistle to the Hebrews.

Let's suppose that when their plan to remodel Solomon's Colonnade and oust the believers from their meeting place in the Temple failed, the Sadducean chief priests employed ecclesiastical power to banish the disciples of Yeshua from participation in the Temple. We can infer this development from the contents of the Epistle to the Hebrews. The community to whom the exhortation is addressed seems to be facing mounting social pressure to renounce their faith in the Master. The epistle frequently enjoins them not to "shrink back" but to hold fast to their faith in Yeshua of Nazareth. The "hall of fame of faith" in Hebrews 11 provides examples of biblical heroes who persevered despite their circumstances and urges the readers to stand fast with the same conviction. The exhorter wrote to the Jewish believers, "Consider Him who has endured such hostility by sinners against Himself, so that you will not grow weary and lose heart" (Hebrews 12:3 NASB). He reminded them of the early days when the community had suffered persecution after the stoning of Stephen:

> Recall the former days when, after you were enlightened, you endured a hard struggle with sufferings, sometimes being publicly exposed to reproach and affliction, and sometimes being partners with those so treated. For you had compassion on those in prison, and you joyfully accepted

the plundering of your property, since you knew that you yourselves had a better possession and an abiding one. Therefore do not throw away your confidence, which has a great reward. (Hebrews 10:32-35)

It seems possible that the Sadducean leadership attempted to place the disciples under the ban (*karet*), cutting them off from the people of Israel. Under the force of the ban, the disciples would have lost access to the Temple and the sacrificial system. The Temple leadership may have formulated the ban to remain in effect only so long as the disciples clung to their confession of Yeshua. To return to fellowship within the Temple, they merely needed to renounce their faith in the Crucified One.

Loss of access to the Temple would have precipitated an enormous spiritual crisis for the early Jewish believers—one far beyond the question of where they would gather. How would they keep the biblical festivals or observe their Levitical obligations? How would they participate in the prayers and sacrifices? How would they prosper in God's blessings on Israel if the priesthood no longer represented them in the presence of God? What would be the consequence of exclusion from the annual ceremony carried out on the Day of Atonement? The entire religious expression of the Jewish people orbited around the Temple and its Levitical services. To be shut out from the Temple must have felt like being cut off from God.

The Heavenly Sanctuary

Banned from the assembly in the Temple, some of the disciples despaired of gathering with other believers at all. The exhorter encouraged them, "Let us hold fast the confession of our hope without wavering, for he who promised is faithful ... not neglecting to meet together, as is the habit of some" (Hebrews 10:23-25).

The exhorter addresses the concerns of the disenfranchised community by discoursing eloquently on the theme of the spiritual priesthood of Messiah in the heavenly Temple. The exhorter reminds his readers that the Jerusalem Temple reflects a higher, heavenly Sanctuary not made with hands. He argues that the Aaronic priesthood reflects the heavenly angelic priesthood and that the high priest on earth corresponds to Messiah's position within the heavenly Temple, where he is seated at the right hand of Glory. By virtue of their allegiance to Yeshua, the disciples have access to those surpassing heavenly realities and need not despair over losing access to the Temple on earth.

Supersessionist interpretation has misconstrued the writer's intention as an argument against participation in the Levitical sacrifices of the Jerusalem Temple and an admonition against backsliding into Judaism. On the contrary, I am suggesting that the writer of the epistle attempted to encourage the Jewish believers to persist in their Yeshua faith even though the Levitical priesthood had turned against them and excluded them from the Temple and the sacrificial system:

> We have an altar from which those who serve the tabernacle have no right to eat. (Hebrews 13:10)

Contrary to popular interpretation, the exhorter did not delegitimize the Temple or the sacrificial system. Instead, he readily admitted, "The blood of goats and bulls and the ashes of a heifer sprinkling those who have been defiled sanctify for the cleansing of the flesh" (Hebrews 9:13 NASB). His readers no longer had access to the blood of goats and bulls and the ashes of a heifer. He told them not to let that dissuade them from their faith in Yeshua:

> How much more will the blood of Messiah, who through the eternal Spirit offered Himself without blemish to God, cleanse your conscience from dead works to serve the living God? (Hebrews 9:14 NASB)

In his theology, the Temple on earth, the Aaronic priesthood, and the Levitical sacrifices that must be continually offered pertain only to atonement within this present world and the earthly Sanctuary. The heavenly Temple above, the messianic high priesthood of Yeshua, and the efficacy of his death, resurrection, ascension, and priestly ministry provide atonement sufficient for obtaining the resurrection of the dead and life in the World to Come.

Outside the Gate

The exhorter compares the situation of his readers to that of the sin offerings that are burned "outside the camp" and to that of the Master who "suffered outside the gate":

> For the bodies of those animals whose blood is brought into the holy places by the high priest as a sacrifice for sin are burned outside the camp. So [Yeshua] also suffered outside the gate in order to sanctify the people through his own blood. Therefore let us go to him outside the camp and bear the reproach he endured. (Hebrews 13:11-13)

He reminds his readers that Jerusalem on earth is only a temporary city, and he turns their attention to the New Jerusalem of the Messianic Era and the World to Come: "Here we have no lasting city, but we seek the city that is to come" (Hebrews 13:14). He encourages them to offer prayers as a substitute for the sacrifices: "Let us continually offer up a sacrifice of praise to God, that is, the fruit of lips that acknowledge his name" (Hebrews 13:15). (After the destruction of the Temple, the rabbis proposed the same principle of substitution based on the same proof text from Hosea 14:2.) Finally, he encourages them to compensate for the omission of sacrifice by the performance of good deeds and acts of lovingkindness: "Do not neglect to do good and to share what you have, for such sacrifices are pleasing to God" (Hebrews 13:16).

The evidence presented above from the Epistle to the Hebrews suggests that shortly after the stoning of James the Righteous, the Sadducean priesthood excommunicated Yeshua's disciples from participation in the Temple services. Our Master had predicted, "They will make you outcasts from the synagogue," i.e., from the assembly (John 16:2 NASB). The blow struck at the heart of the community and shook the disciples deeply.

The ban also had the effect of removing the intercessory prayers of Yeshua's disciples from the Temple, opening the gates of the Temple to its impending doom: "See, your house is left to you desolate" (Matthew 23:38).

This reconstruction of the theological and social crisis that inspired the composition of the epistle helps make sense of its contents without resorting to supersessionism or an obviation of the Torah. It preserves the integrity of the New Testament, which depicts the Apostolic-era disciples actively engaged in the Temple and its worship system, and it offers a way to read and understand the epistle in a manner consistent with Messianic Jewish convictions.

The Remedy before the Wound

I have argued that the epistle seems to have been written before the Jewish war with Rome began. Nevertheless, from a spiritual perspective, it seems to me as if God intended the epistle to prepare his people for that event. By expounding upon the priesthood of Yeshua, his sacrificial death, the Temple not made with hands, and the heavenly Jerusalem, the exhorter unknowingly prepared his readers for a long and miserable exile without priesthood, without sacrifice, without Temple, and without the holy city of Jerusalem. The Epistle to the Hebrews warned the disciples of Yeshua against despair, and it encouraged them to stand fast even in the absence of the Temple. Curiously, this epistle seems to have been written only a few years before the current exile began, shortly before the seven-year interval between the start of the revolt against Rome and the fall of Masada. In the middle of these seven years came the destruction of Jerusalem and the Temple and the annulment of the priestly service. The book of Hebrews almost seems to anticipate those events and the great tribulation that would soon take place under the tread of Roman boots.

Grant Luton, the teaching pastor at Beth Tikkun in Ohio, offered a profound insight into the spiritual function of the Epistle to the Hebrews. He quoted the rabbinic maxim that says, "Before the Holy One, blessed be he, inflicts the wound, he prepares the remedy" (b.*Megillah* 13b). The Epistle to the Hebrews offers the remedy, teaching the Jewish people how to sustain themselves in the absence of the priesthood, sacrifices, Temple, and holy city. The Epistle to the Hebrews offers not just comfort and consolation but also a remedy in the form of instructions for bringing the exile to an end.

None of this would have been apparent to the first readers of the epistle nor even to the exhorter himself, but after the destruction of the Temple and the fall of Jerusalem, this word of exhortation became brilliantly relevant. In retrospect, it seems as if God sent this word of exhortation to the Jewish people on the eve of destruction—on the eve of the longest, darkest exile that the Jewish people have ever known.

CHAPTER THREE:
SUNDRY TIMES AND DIVERS MANNERS
(HEBREWS 1:1–2)

The apostles assigned the same weight to the words of Yeshua as to the words of the Torah and the Prophets.

The book of Hebrews gives readers a front-row seat in a first-century synagogue to hear a teaching from one of the disciples of the original apostles. It reads much like a piece of rabbinic literature, such as the Midrash, parts of the Talmud, or the mystical *Zohar*. It follows an entirely rabbinic style of dissertation, using esoteric allusions to the Hebrew Scriptures similar to the type the rabbis enjoyed, taking passages out of their apparent context and furnishing them with new significance similar to the way the sages often did. The exhorter responsible for this exhortation advances his argument with sudden departures from the linear thought to which we are accustomed, making broad sweeps of logic and exploiting obscure nuances in biblical texts before returning to the original point.

I feel at home in the book of Hebrews because I have spent a lot of time reading rabbinic literature, but I feel sorry for the uninitiated and unsuspecting Bible reader who steps unwarily into this type of material. My children grew up with this kind of Bible study and dabbled in the rabbinic texts, so my oldest son, Isaac, while taking a class on talmudic argumentation at Hebrew University in Jerusalem, found it amusing to observe the startled reaction of other students as they experienced their first encounters with the seemingly bizarre logic of the rabbis. Isaac compared it to the cognitive equivalent of stepping on a rake. As we proceed through the book of Hebrews, I will do my best to guide the way lest we suffer the same consequence.

Long ago, at many times and in many ways, God spoke. (HEBREWS 1:1)

The book of Hebrews opens with a statement on God's mode of revelation. In the past, God spoke to his people through various means and methods. More recently, the voice of God has spoken through the agency of his Son, Yeshua:

> Long ago, at many times and in many ways, God spoke to our fathers by the prophets, but in these last days he has spoken to us by his Son. (Hebrews 1:1–2)

The King James Version puts it more poetically: "God, who at sundry times and in divers manners spake in time past unto the fathers by the prophets." In simpler words, "God spoke through the writers of the Bible."

The Jewish Bible is called the Tanach. That name is an acronym derived from the threefold division of the Bible: the **T**orah (the Torah), the **N**evi'im (the Prophets), and the **K**etuvim (the Writings).

- **T**: Torah (Law)
- **N**: Nevi'im (Prophets)
- **K**: Ketuvim (Writings)

When the exhorter says "the prophets," he has in mind the writers of the Scriptures and several key figures in the Scriptures. The list of "the prophets" would include Abraham, Isaac, Jacob, and especially Moses. As the author of the Torah and the greatest of the prophets, Moses represents the Torah. In Jewish Bibles, the books of the rest of the prophets come subsequent to and rank below the Torah. They include the major and minor prophetic books as well as the historical books written by prophets such as Joshua, Judges, 1 and 2 Samuel, and 1 and 2 Kings.

The exhorter also refers to the Writings, the Ketuvim, such as Psalms, Proverbs, and Song of Songs, written by inspired men like King David and King Solomon. The Jewish people believed that the Psalms and the Writings were inspired by the Spirit of the LORD.

Properly understood, the first verse of the book of Hebrews makes reference to the Torah, the Nevi'im, and Ketuvim—the whole Tanach—which Christians now refer to as the Old Testament. In the Apostolic Era, and at the time of the writing of the book of Hebrews, these books constituted the entirety of sacred Scripture; there was, as yet, no New Testament.

The message here is that God inspired the Bible, the Tanach, by speaking to and through men of God. He spoke at many times and in many ways, which brings to mind a passage in Numbers:

> If there is a prophet among you, I the LORD make myself known to him in a vision; I speak with him in a dream ... in riddles ... not so with my servant Moses ... with him I speak mouth to mouth, clearly. (Numbers 12:6-8)

To some God spoke in dreams. To some he spoke in visions. To some he spoke in riddles and oracles. To Moses he spoke directly and clearly. Through these "divers manners," he spoke the Bible that we call "God's Word." It contains the oracles of the living God, the words of his prophets, and his communication with his people Israel.

In these last days. (HEBREWS 1:2)

In the past, God spoke through his prophets by various means. All this was obvious to the original readers of the Epistle to the Hebrews, but the argument moves from the established point and proposes that "in these last days he has spoken to us by his Son" (Hebrews 1:2).

The phrase "in these last days" indicates that the apostles believed they were living in the last days. They knew that the culmination of the age was at hand because the good news of the gospel proclaimed it to be so. This was the very message of the gospel they had heard spoken to them by the Son and to which they had dedicated their own lives, proclaiming, "The kingdom of heaven is at hand."

From our perspective these many centuries later, it is easy to feel cynical about those unfortunate, naïve fellows who thought they were living in the last days. Here we are two thousand years later, still waiting for the last days. On the contrary, the apostles *were* living in the last days of *their* generation, of which the Master said, "*This generation* will not pass away until these things are accomplished." In their immediate future lay the end of the Second Temple Era. They believed that unless the nation repented according to the teaching of Yeshua, they would soon see the fall of Jerusalem and the destruction of the Temple, the war of Gog and Magog, the great tribulation, the revelation of the antichrist, and the abomination of desolation. They anticipated the hoped-for glorious appearance of the Son of Man within their generation. The course of history deferred that hope. We still wait for the return of the Master. Nevertheless, the generation of the apostles actually lived through a preliminary version of several of the principal events just described. Those events indeed pointed toward the last days. In that respect, we have been on the edge of those "last days" now for nearly two thousand years.

He has spoken to us by his Son. (HEBREWS 1:2)

Remember when you had to write a paper in your senior year or freshman composition class, and the teacher made you begin it with a thesis statement? I disliked that. I prefer to launch right into the writing and let the reader figure out my thesis all on his own. But a good writer begins by stating his thesis up front. Hebrews 1:1-2 provides the thesis statement for the book of Hebrews:

> In the past, God spoke through the writers and characters of the Bible, but in these last days, he spoke through his Son.

That's the heart of the whole Epistle to the Hebrews. It means that the words and teachings of Yeshua of Nazareth were, to his disciples, like Scripture itself. They were not merely inspiring thoughts or commentary on the Torah—rather, they were the Word of God, as Peter said:

> Master, to whom shall we go? You have the words of eternal life, and we have believed, and have come to know, that you are the Holy One of God. (John 6:68-69)

The rest of the book of Hebrews attempts to prove that premise. Christian New Testament readers often read right past that thesis without appreciating its significance because Christian-published Bibles make it seem pretty obvious that the Gospels and the words of Jesus are on the level of Scripture and part of the Bible, as are the writings of the apostles and even the book of Hebrews itself. They are all part of our Bible, and the canon has been closed for a long time. But let's slow down and think about the statement from a first-century Jewish perspective. In their world, they also had a canon. The Hebrew Scriptures comprised the Tanach; there was no New Testament. To say that God was still speaking to the world as he did in the days of the biblical prophets required a radical leap. To say that he was now speaking to the world exclusively through Yeshua of Nazareth was even more radical. It would be somewhat akin to me saying that in the past, God spoke through the writers of the Bible, but in our day, he has spoken to us through C.S. Lewis or Billy Graham. Such a statement would invite controversy because it would be elevating Lewis or Graham to a level of authority equal to the Bible. Likewise, for the original Jewish readers of the epistle, the exhorter's radical opening statement demanded a defending argument if it was to stand.

The statement indicates that the apostles assigned the same weight to the words of Yeshua as they did to the words of the forefathers, Abraham, Isaac, Jacob, Moses, and the prophets. This premise explains why the exhorter must demonstrate that the Messiah is higher than the priesthood, higher than the patriarchs, higher than Moses, and higher even than the angels. He attempts to validate his opening thesis statement with several chapters of supporting argumentation. Along the way, he reveals the implications of his premise. If it is true that in these last days, God has spoken to us through his Son in a manner that carries the same authority (or more) as the prophets of the past, then we had better listen and not turn our backs on what the Son has to say. We had better be careful not to fall away from him. This is the warning and overall message of the book of Hebrews. However, the exhorter makes several excursions from that central point as he meanders through his word of exhortation.

Exaltation of Messiah

> Behold, my servant shall act wisely; he shall be high and lifted up, and shall be [exceedingly] exalted. (Isaiah 52:13)

Isaiah's song of the suffering servant begins with a statement about the exalted status of the servant of the LORD. An early Aramaic version of the Bible called *Targum Yonatan* paraphrases, saying, "Behold, my servant the Messiah shall prosper, he shall be exalted and extolled." Isaiah describes the exaltation of the servant of the LORD in three expressions. The servant will be

- high (*yarum*),
- lifted up (*nisa*),
- and greatly exalted (*gavah me'od*).

An early and once well-known explanation (midrash) of this passage explains that Isaiah 52:13 speaks of Messiah's exaltation above the forefathers, above Moses, and even above the angels. That sequence sounds similar to the opening chapters of the book of Hebrews. This explanation appears in numerous sources, with many variations on the same theme. Even Rashi cited the messianic exaltation as a valid alternative to his own thoughts on Isaiah 52:13. The midrash plays on the Hebrew words for "high" (*rum*), "lifted up" (*nasa*), and "exalted" (*gavah*), finding a corresponding form of each word in reference to Abraham, Moses, and the angels respectively:

- King Messiah is greater than the patriarchs, as it is said [in Isaiah 52:13], "My servant will be high and lifted up and greatly exalted." Higher than Abraham, who says [in Genesis 14:22], "I have raised my hand *high* to the LORD."
- King Messiah is lifted up above Moses, to whom it is said [in Numbers 11:12], "*Lift* it to your bosom."
- King Messiah is more exalted than the ministering angels, of whom it is written [in Ezekiel 1:18], "As for their rims they were *exalted* and awesome." And out of whom does he come forth? From David. (*Yalkut Shimoni II* 571)

Students of rabbinic literature could cite numerous similar examples to prove that the early sages regarded the servant of the LORD in Isaiah 52-53 as the Messiah. The *Zohar* also offers a similar interpretation in reference to Messiah:

> "Behold, my servant will prosper, he will be *high and lifted up and greatly exalted*" (Isaiah 52:13). He will be *high*, above the upper light of all the luminaries, as it is written [in Isaiah 30:18], "He waits on *high* to have compassion on you." He will be *lifted up* above Abraham, *high* above Isaac, *greatly exalted* above Jacob ... All the dead who are in the dust will then awake. This is the mystery of "My Servant" in whose hands are the keys of his Master, as were Abraham's in those of Eliezer. (*Zohar, Vayeshev* 1:181b)

The book of Hebrews offers similar thoughts on the exaltation of Messiah when it says, "He sat down at the right hand of the Majesty on high, having become so much better than the angels, as He has inherited a more excellent name than they" (Hebrews 1:3-4 NASB), and when he says that he "has been counted worthy of more glory than Moses" (Hebrews 3:3).

The emphasis on the exaltation of the Messiah becomes clear at the beginning of Hebrews 2, where we are warned to pay close attention "to what we have heard, lest we drift away." That is to say, we should pay close attention to the words of Yeshua:

> Therefore we must pay much closer attention to what we have heard, lest we drift away from it. For since the message declared by angels proved to be reliable, and every transgression or disobedience received a just retribution, how shall we escape if we neglect such a great salvation? (Hebrews 2:1-3)

"What we have heard" refers to the message and teaching of the Son through whom God is speaking with us. We "must pay much closer attention" to the words of Yeshua. In those words, God is speaking to us, just as he spoke to his people through Moses and all the prophets in the past. Today, he is speaking through his Son.

CHAPTER FOUR:
RADIANCE OF GLORY
(HEBREWS 1:1-3)

The Son of God is superior to the prophets and the angels because he is the manifestation of the Divine Wisdom and the image of God.

The book of Hebrews commences with a provocative premise. In the past, God spoke through the characters and writers of the Tanach, the Old Testament, "but in these last days he has spoken to us by his Son" (Hebrews 1:2). By putting forward such a premise at the outset, the exhorter weighs Yeshua against the patriarchs, Abraham, Isaac, and Jacob, and the Torah of Moses (which was given through angels) and finds Yeshua in no way the inferior. For the rest of the chapter and into the next, he works to support his premise that the Son is superior to the prophets, superior to Moses, and superior to the angels, as the midrash on Isaiah 52:13 extrapolates: "The Messiah shall be high and lifted up and exceedingly exalted: higher than Abraham, lifted above Moses, exceedingly exalted above the angels."

The Image of the Father

One of my children once asked incredulously, "How can Jesus be God? Isn't he the Son of God?" How would you answer that question? That's what the field of Christology is all about. Christology is a word that means the study of Christ, the study of Messiah, particularly concerning his divine nature. The opening chapters of the book of Hebrews offer a quick study on the subject. It's a topic generally neglected in our day because popular Christian culture takes it for granted that Jesus is God to the point of completely obscuring the distinction between the Father and Son and conflating each with the other. Thanks to the Father-Son confusion prevalent in the church, popular Christian music and conventional prayer forms rarely distinguish between the two. Father and Son are carelessly homogenized, and it is generally taken for granted, for example, that God died on the cross for your sins.

Father-Son confusion is nothing new. According to the Talmud, the Holy One, blessed be he, wanted to ensure that everyone knew Abraham was Isaac's legitimate father. How could this be accomplished? God made the face of the child Isaac like a mirror image of his father, Abraham. When people looked at the son, it was as if they were looking at the father. The Talmud says, "The lines of Isaac's face looked like Abraham's, and they all cried out, 'Abraham begat Isaac'" (b.*Bava Metzia* 87a). They knew that Isaac was truly Abraham's son because father and son looked so much alike that people could not tell them apart in later years. God had to introduce the aging process into the world so that we could distinguish the elder from the younger. Before that, the legend says, "Whoever wished to speak to Abraham spoke to Isaac, and whoever wished to speak to Isaac spoke to Abraham." The talmudic legend brings to mind the Master's words: "Whoever has seen me has seen the Father" (John 14:9).

Deep Mysteries

The first chapter of Hebrews comes tightly packed with apostolic thought, assumption, and interpretation. We will recognize ideas found in the schools of the apostles and also from the broader world of Jewish and rabbinic thought. It is not propositional material. The exhorter is not introducing theological innovations. He speaks from a position of authority and authoritative tradition.

Some scholars believe that this first chapter—or portions of this first chapter—might have originally functioned as a liturgical element employed by first-century Jewish believers. Alternatively, and more likely, portions of this first chapter quoted a well-known but long-since forgotten collection of apostolic midrashim (expositions), echoes of which we find in the Gospel of John and the first chapter of Paul's epistle to the Colossians. If this alternate suggestion is *not* true, then at the very least, Hebrews seems to share some common oral sources with those passages.

This chapter also provides a relatively early example of Jewish mysticism—a catalog of ideas that, according to the Talmud, we should not be allowed to study until we are over the age of forty, and even then, only in whispers, not spoken out loud. Thanks to the revelation of Yeshua, the concealed is revealed, as our Master says: "Nothing is covered that will not be revealed or hidden that will not be known" (Matthew 10:26).

The task at hand is not one of reinventing Christology or undermining church doctrine. The Trinity is not up for reexamination in Hebrews 1–2. Our task is to better understand how the exhorter (and the broader apostolic community) arrived at the high Christology expressed in the first two chapters of the epistle while staying within the theological boundaries of Jewish monotheism.

Right out of the gate, the exhorter begins our initiation into the deep mysteries of Messiah. Within the first three verses, we are plunged deep into ontological musings about his divine nature:

> Long ago, at many times and in many ways, God spoke to our fathers by the prophets, but in these last days he has spoken to us by his Son, whom he appointed the heir of all things, through whom also he created the world. He is the radiance of the glory of God and the exact imprint of his nature, and he upholds the universe by the word of his power. (Hebrews 1:1–3)

Whom he appointed the heir of all things. (HEBREWS 1:2)

God has made the Son the heir of all things. In ancient Jewish culture, a "son" was a man's heir—particularly the firstborn son because he received a double portion of the inheritance. He inherited the birthright, the blessing, and the headship over the family. For example, Abraham complained that he had no heir to inherit his possessions and the promises God had given him. The LORD had promised a son named Isaac, who became the heir. And, as mentioned above, the sages teach that to validate Isaac's claim to the inheritance, the LORD made Isaac look exactly like Abraham.

The exhorter indicates that one reason the Messiah is called "God's Son" is that God makes the Messiah heir of all things. In the kingdom of heaven and the World to Come, the Almighty will place all things in subjugation to the Messiah (Psalm 2:8). As Paul said,

> When all things are subjected to him (the Son), then the Son himself will also be subjected to him (the Father) who put all things in subjection under him, that God may be all in all. (1 Corinthians 15:28)

Why does God appoint the Son as heir to all things? Because all things were made through the Son, "whom he appointed the heir of all things, through whom also he created the world" (Hebrews 1:2).

Through whom also he created the world. (HEBREWS 1:2)

God created the world through the Son. This statement should cause us to object, "What's going on here? Does the Bible say, 'In the beginning, Jesus created the heavens and the earth?'" It does not. The idea of Jesus as the Creator is problematic. The mental image it conjures simultaneously diminishes the transcendent, unbegotten God, who spoke and by whom all things came into existence, and it also diminishes the humanity of Yeshua of Nazareth. My mind imagines a coloring-book Jesus, clad in white robes, hovering over the nothingness of the void, saying: "Let there be ...."

That's not how the apostles intended us to understand Yeshua's role in creating the heavens and the earth. Hebrews 1:2 does not say, "Jesus created all things." It says, "Through him God created the world." But according to the Torah, God created the world *through* his spoken word. He said, "*y'hi or* (Let there be light)," and "*vayehi or* (There was light)." He created all things through his spoken Word (Aramaic: *Memra*; Greek: *Logos*). Based on this idea, the apostles taught that God created all things through the Son, who is the Word made flesh.

On the surface, this does not sound like a Jewish notion at all. It sounds like more Father-Son confusion. However, if we look closely, we discover that this theological postulate is solidly based on ideas found in ancient Jewish mysticism. If we compare it with other teachings in the New Testament, we discover that this theology of creation through divine agency was a critical and central concept in apostolic Christology.

The ancient sages taught that God created the universe through the agency of his wisdom, and when God created the heavens and the earth, he did so through an agent, like a man who hires a building contractor to build a house. You might create the blueprints and the design of your house down to the smallest detail, but then you turn those designs over to a contractor, and he executes the plan. The sages suggested that God used a contractor when he built the heavens and the earth.

This idea comes directly from Proverbs 3:19: "The LORD by *wisdom* founded the earth." Wisdom is the contractor God hired to execute his designs. Proverbs 8 personifies God's wisdom and even claims that she (Wisdom) was present at the time of the creation as the master workman at God's side. (In Hebrew, "wisdom" is the feminine noun *chochmah*, which takes a feminine pronoun.) Wisdom declares,

> The LORD possessed me at the beginning of His way, before His works of old. From everlasting I was established, from the beginning, from the earliest times of the earth. (Proverbs 8:22-23 NASB)

She says that she was present with God before the depths existed, before the mountains, before the earth, before the waters above, before the waters below, and before the heavens. She says, "I was beside Him, as a master workman; and I was daily His delight, rejoicing always before Him" (Proverbs 8:30 NASB).

Poetry like Proverbs 8 speaks in abstractions, not in concrete terms. Jewish mysticism speaks in the language of metaphor and symbol. Mental images are not always helpful when discussing esoteric truths, and there is always a danger in taking anthropomorphisms literally. In this case, whatever mental image this passage creates, it will be a wrong impression if we picture God's wisdom as a separate person. God's wisdom is not separate from him any more than your thoughts are separate from you. God's wisdom is part of him but not the whole of him. The attribute of *chochmah* is not the totality of his transcendent being, but neither is it not him.

The rabbis saw correspondences between Genesis 1:1 and the wisdom passages in which Wisdom speaks in the first person. They noticed that the Bible seems to link wisdom and the first Hebrew word of Genesis together. The first Hebrew word of Genesis is *Bereshit*, "In the beginning." Notice the following correlations:

> In the beginning [*bereshit*], God created the heavens and the earth. (Genesis 1:1)

> The fear of the LORD is the beginning [*reshit*] of wisdom. (Psalm 111:10)

> The LORD possessed me [wisdom] at the beginning [*reshit*] of His way, before His works of old. (Proverbs 8:22 NASB)

It looks like Wisdom was present at the beginning. Genesis 1:1 says God created *bereshit*, meaning "in the beginning," but Proverbs 3:19 says, "*b'chochmah*, in wisdom," the LORD founded the earth. The ancient Jewish paraphrases of the Bible make these associations between the supernal wisdom and the creation narrative explicit. They depict wisdom as a co-creator with God:

> From the beginning, with wisdom the LORD created and perfected the heavens and the earth. (Genesis 1:1, *Targum Neofiti*)

> In wisdom the LORD created. (Genesis 1:1, *Targum Yerushalmi*)

This is how the apostles were taught the Torah. Although the written Targums did not yet exist, the apostles lived in a world of targumic paraphrases. That association also explains the opening words of the Gospel of John: "In the beginning the *Logos* was with God and was God and all things are created through the *Logos*." If John meant "wisdom personified" when he said *Logos*, we might understand the first three verses of his gospel as follows:

> In the beginning was the [divine wisdom,] and the [divine wisdom] was with God, and the [divine wisdom] was God. [The divine wisdom] was in the beginning with God. All things were made through [divine wisdom], and without [the divine wisdom] was not any thing made that was made. (John 1:1–3 paraphrase)

He is the radiance of the glory of God. (HEBREWS 1:3)

The New Testament explicitly refers to Yeshua as "the wisdom of God" (1 Corinthians 1:24). Paul said, "We speak God's wisdom in a mystery, the hidden wisdom which God predestined before the ages to our glory" (1 Corinthians 2:7 NASB). He speaks of a secret wisdom that preexisted creation. What is the mystical, hidden wisdom that existed before the ages? We can turn to extrabiblical literature to help establish the religious and cultural context for this idea.

The apostles were familiar with the deuterocanonical book titled the *Book of Wisdom*, sometimes called *Wisdom of Solomon*. The New Testament alludes to it, and Clement of Rome quotes from it. The expositor appears to allude to *Wisdom of Solomon* as he invokes wisdom-mysticism to describe the Son of God. *Wisdom of Solomon* contains a passage that may have been of enormous importance to the apostles as they tried to understand the divine and human nature of our Master to define their own Christology.

In this passage, King Solomon, the son of David, is speaking, but when we read it from an apostolic perspective, we can hear the passage as a prophetic forecasting of the voice of Yeshua, who, like King Solomon, is called the Son of David:

> I myself also am a mortal man, like to all, and the offspring of him that was first made of the earth, and in my mother's womb was fashioned to be flesh in the time of ten months, being compacted in blood, of the seed of man, and the pleasure that came with sleep. And when I was born, I drew in the common air, and fell upon the earth, which is of like nature, and the first voice which I uttered was crying, as all others do. I was nursed in swaddling clothes, and that with cares. For there is no king that had any other beginning of birth. For all men have one entrance into life, and the like going out. Wherefore I prayed, and understanding was given me: I called upon God, and the spirit of wisdom came to me. I preferred her before sceptres and thrones, and esteemed riches nothing in comparison of her. (*Wisdom of Solomon* 7:1-8, King James Apocrypha)

When the king says, "The spirit of wisdom came to me," the apostles would have understood that spiritual endowment in view of the messianic prophecy in Isaiah that says, "The Spirit of the LORD shall rest upon him [the Messiah], the Spirit of wisdom and understanding, the Spirit of counsel and might, the Spirit of knowledge and the fear of the LORD" (Isaiah 11:2). Further down in the *Wisdom* passage, the king extols the spirit of wisdom that has come to rest upon him:

> For wisdom, which is the worker of all things, taught me: for in her is an understanding holy spirit ... For wisdom is more moving than any motion: she passeth and goeth through all things by reason of her pureness. For she is the breath of the power of God, and a pure influence flowing from the glory of the Almighty: therefore can no defiled thing fall into her. For she is the brightness of the everlasting light, the unspotted mirror of the power of God, and the image of his goodness. And being but one, she can do all things: and remaining in herself, she maketh all things new: and in all ages entering into holy souls, she maketh them friends of God, and prophets. (*Wisdom of Solomon* 7:22, 24-27 KJA)

> She [wisdom] is an initiate in the knowledge of God, and an associate in his works. (*Wisdom of Solomon* 8:4)

> By your wisdom you have formed humankind. (*Wisdom of Solomon* 9:2)

Let's summarize what these passages from *Wisdom of Solomon* say about the divine wisdom:

1. She is the worker of all things.
2. She passes through and goes through all things, holding them together.
3. She is the breath and power of God.
4. She is an expression of the glory of the Almighty.
5. She is the brightness of everlasting light.
6. She is the image of God's goodness.
7. She makes all things new.

We are trading in the same kind of currency when we read in Hebrews, "He is the radiance of the glory of God and the exact imprint of his nature, and he upholds the universe by the word of his power" (Hebrews 1:3).

The exact imprint of his nature. (HEBREWS 1:3)

The New Testament applies these Jewish ideas about wisdom—her relation to God and her role in creation—to the Son. The divine wisdom is in him, and the Son is the expression of the wisdom of God. Paul employs these concepts in his epistle to the Colossians:

> He is the image of the invisible God, the firstborn of all creation. For by him all things were created, in heaven and on earth, visible and invisible, whether thrones or dominions or rulers or authorities—all things were created through him and for him. And he is before all things, and in him all things hold together. (Colossians 1:15-17)

Notice the close correspondence between this passage and Hebrews 1:3. Paul says, "He is the image of the invisible God." The book of Hebrews says he is "the exact imprint of his nature." Two expressions for the same concept. He is the image of God, as it says in the Torah: "God created man in his own image, in the image of God he created him" (Genesis 1:27). God made Adam in his image, but the Son *is* the image of God. This implies that the first human being, Adam, is an earthly correspondence to the heavenly Adam, the image of God, the eternal Adam:

> As was the man [Adam] of dust, so also are those who are of the dust, and as is the man of heaven, so also are those who are of heaven. Just as we have borne the image of the man of dust, we shall also bear the image of the man of heaven. (1 Corinthians 15:48-49)

The Messiah shall be high and lifted up and exceedingly exalted because the Spirit of the LORD shall rest upon him, that is, the spirit of wisdom. The spirit of divine wisdom (the *Logos*) tabernacled in him. In Yeshua the heavenly Adam (the image of God) was united with the earthly Adam (who was made in the image of God). In Yeshua the heavenly pattern merged into the earthly copy.

Wisdom Made Flesh

The Chasidic master Rabbi Levi Yitzchak of Berditchev said that what made him fall in love with Chasidut was that the Maggid of Mezeritch taught Jewish mysticism as if it was *musar* (ethics and moral discipline). In other words, it was never just ideas for the sake of ideas, never just speculating about God for the sake of speculation; it always had practical life application.

The same principle applies here. Our theological inquiry into the incarnation of the divine wisdom has practical application. The writer of the book of Hebrews brings the lesson home:

> Therefore we must pay much closer attention to what we have heard, lest we drift away from it. (Hebrews 2:1)

Pay much closer attention to the gospel, the teaching of Yeshua, and his declaration about the kingdom of heaven.

It is the job of every disciple of Yeshua to bring the divine wisdom into unity with our own selves, our bodies, our families, our communities, humanity, and all creation. We strive to build a tabernacle where he might dwell among and within us. Our Master said, "Every disciple fully trained will be like his master." Therefore, our training as disciples involves bringing down this divine wisdom, bringing the spirit of wisdom into the world by becoming a vessel for the divine wisdom just as our Master was the incarnation of it.

If the disciples of Yeshua constitute the body of Messiah, we should also be the tabernacle of the *Logos*, the divine wisdom made flesh, and there are practical ways that we can become so. First of all, as the writer of the book of Hebrews says, "Pay much closer attention," because in the past, "God spoke to our fathers by the prophets, but in these last days he has spoken to us by his Son." The words of our teacher, Yeshua of Nazareth, communicate the spirit of wisdom. Our job is to eat of the bread of life and drink of the living water, internalizing his teaching and then living it out. This happens in the spheres of thought, speech, and deed. Write them on your heart; speak of them when you walk in the way; do them. "Say to wisdom, 'You are my sister,' and call insight your intimate friend" (Proverbs 7:4).

When we keep the commandments of God, we bring him into the world in the flesh, so to speak. This is what it means to be "Christlike"—to import the revelation of godliness from the coming kingdom into this current age, to wrap the Torah and the gospel in flesh by becoming agents of that revelation. Then we who are made in the image of God will be united with the image of God.

CHAPTER FIVE:
TEN TESTIMONIES
(HEBREWS 1:3–2:18)

A chain of ten linking proof texts
demonstrates the Messiah's superiority
over angels and establishes his authority.

The first two chapters of the book of Hebrews consist of a rapid-fire series of proof texts, strung one after another like links in a chain, to prove the Messiah's superiority over angels. It's not your typical Bible study.

Apostolic Bible Study

Apostolic-style Bible study, that is, rabbinic-style exegesis, is unlike the standard methods of Bible learning to which we might be accustomed today. Typical Bible studies today involve reading, reflection, and searching for a personal application or for promises to claim. Sometimes you might be encouraged to study at a deeper level, spending time trying to determine the historical, grammatical, and literary contexts for the author's meaning, intention, and audience. The type of Bible study the apostles did was nothing like that. If you read my previous books in this series, *The Holy Epistle to the Galatians* and *The Holy Epistle to the Ephesians,* you are already marginally familiar with Paul's interpretive style. It's difficult to decipher, obscure, and extremely rabbinic, but we should remember that Paul was writing to God-fearing Gentile believers who were relatively new to the Scriptures. He wrote at a level appropriate for their understanding. Conversely, here in

Hebrews, we have an apostolic-level author writing an exhortation to Jewish readers who are thoroughly immersed in the Scriptures and accustomed to rabbinic forms of dissertation.

One of those forms of dissertation is called *midrash*. The word *midrash* comes from the Hebrew word *darash*, which means "to search." Midrashic Bible study typically builds on a series of proof texts. Everything must be established from the Scriptures. We frequently encounter phrases like "as it is written" and "as it is said." In Hebrews 1-2, we will examine ten proof texts drawn from the Torah, the Prophets, and the Writings.

Before we begin, it's essential to remember that there were no chapter and verse divisions in the days of the apostles. Scrolls unrolled in a continuous stream of text. Consequently, Jewish scholars were compelled to refer to passages by quoting a short section, a few words, or even just a single word from a text to refer to a passage. This method gave rise to the names of our weekly Torah portions. Basic Jewish primary school education involved memorization of the Hebrew Scriptures. This enabled an educated Jew to invoke a text of Scripture by quoting just a few keywords or a short passage extracted from it. It is easy to miss the intention of the exhorter if we read only the short bit he quotes without examining the context of the passage of Scripture to which his short quotation might be alluding.

We should also remember that midrash is typically built on a series of word associations and other hermeneutical principles that make very little sense to our Western minds. Rabbinic hermeneutics rest on the foundation that all Scripture is God-breathed and inspired, down to the smallest jot and tittle. God has deliberately placed every word and letter. This conviction led to methods of biblical interpretation in which the sages might dissect a passage, link its components to otherwise disparate passages based on specific keywords, and put them back together to arrive at new understandings of the text. This form of interpretation is found throughout Jewish history and is still taught in rabbinic seminaries today. We find the same rabbinic model for interpreting the Bible at work in the Mishnah, the Talmud, and the writings of the apostles of Yeshua.

After making purification for sins. (HEBREWS 1:3)

The "purification for sins" accomplished by Yeshua is the subject of study in later chapters of the epistle, particularly Hebrews 9–10. In short, the "purification for sins" accomplished by the Messiah refers to his testing, suffering, death, resurrection, and ascension. His suffering is compared to the sacrificial rites, and his resurrection and ascension to the heavenly Temple are compared to the ministrations of the Aaronic priesthood in the Temple and the presence of God. Yeshua suffered not for his own sins but for the sins of others. These concepts are developed further on in the epistle.

He sat down at the right hand of the Majesty on high. (HEBREWS 1:3)

After completing the work of "making purification for sins," Yeshua ascended to a position of exaltation, taking his seat at the right hand of God, in accord with the ensuing interpretation of Psalm 110:1: "The LORD says to my Lord: 'Sit at my right hand.'" That messianic interpretation of Psalm 110 and the significance of Messiah taking a seat "at the right hand" of God will be explored below in the commentary on Hebrews 1:13 and in more detail in the commentary on Hebrews 4:14.

Having become as much superior to angels. (HEBREWS 1:4)

The author of Hebrews commences on a path of midrashic argumentation to prove his premise that the Son is superior to the angels. In the process, he uses a string of rapid-fire proof texts to establish his point. The texts are neither random in their order nor disassociated from each other. Instead, each text is connected with those before and after it, like links in a chain, leading to the desired conclusion.

It will be helpful, as we attempt to sort through this series of proof texts, to see the objective at the end of the argument: "Now it was not to angels that God subjected the world to come, of which we are speaking" (Hebrews 2:5). In other words, the subject under discussion is the World to Come, and the question brought to the table pertains not to the present age as we see and experience it but instead to the future kingdom era and the ensuing new heavens and new earth. Who will hold authority over the kingdom and the World to Come? The angels, or Yeshua?

As the name he has inherited is more excellent than theirs. (HEBREWS 1:4)

Yeshua holds a position of superiority over the angels, a station indicated by the fact that "the name he has inherited is more excellent than theirs." What is the name that the Son has inherited? One might assume that the name in view is God's name or the powerful name Yeshua. After all, in a similar passage, Paul makes just such a statement:

> God has highly exalted him and bestowed on him the name that is above every name, so that at the name of [Yeshua] every knee should bow, in heaven and on earth and under the earth, and every tongue confess that [Yeshua the Messiah] is Lord. (Philippians 2:9-11)

These were not the names the exhorter had in mind when he spoke of "a name that is higher than angels" and "more excellent than theirs." Instead, the exhorter spoke of the title "Son of God." To support the premise that the title "the Son" is superior to angels, he offers his first in the series of proof texts: "For to which of the angels did God ever say, 'You are my Son, today I have begotten you'?" (Hebrews 1:5).

For to which of the angels did God ever say, "You are my Son, today I have begotten you"? (HEBREWS 1:5)

The exhorter cites Psalm 2 to prove that "Son of God" is an appropriate title for the Messiah. Conventional Jewish interpretation frames Psalm 2 as a messianic psalm about the future war of Gog and Magog and the establishment of the Messianic Kingdom. It contains a conversation between God and his Messiah. In the New Testament, even God himself quotes Psalm 2 regarding the Messiah when, at the immersion of the Master, a voice from heaven was heard to say, "This is My Son." I have printed the full text of the psalm below with brackets [like this] to indicate the conventional Jewish interpretation of the psalm and to make its messianic significance clearer:

> Why do the nations [of Gog and Magog] rage and the peoples plot in vain? The kings of the earth set themselves, and the rulers take counsel together, against the LORD and against his Anointed [the Messiah], saying, "Let us burst their bonds apart and cast away their cords from us [by rebelling against the Messiah]." He who sits in the heavens laughs; the Lord holds them in derision. Then he will speak to them in his wrath, and terrify them in his fury, saying, "As for me, I have set my [Messiah] King on Zion, my holy hill [the place from which Messiah will reign]."
>
> [The Messiah says,] I will tell of the decree: The LORD said to me, "You are my Son; today I have begotten you. Ask of me, and I will make the nations your heritage, and the ends of the earth your possession. You shall break them with a rod of iron and dash them in pieces like a potter's vessel."
>
> Now therefore, O kings, be wise; be warned, O rulers of the earth. Serve the LORD with fear and rejoice with trembling. Kiss the Son, lest he be angry, and you perish in the way, for his wrath is quickly kindled. Blessed are all who take refuge in him. (Psalm 2)

The key verse here is, "You are My Son; today I have begotten you." An early Greek version of this psalm, perhaps also employed by the exhorter, reads, "You are My Son; today I have become your Father." We need to take note of four things:

- "Son of God" is used as a title for the Messiah.
- The Messiah receives the Gentile nations and all the ends of the earth as his possession by an act of inheritance. This is the source for our writer's earlier statement, "His Son, whom he appointed the heir of all things."
- An allusion is made to the Messiah's throne when the psalm says, "I have set my King on Zion, my holy hill."
- Mention is made of Messiah's scepter as a rod of iron with which he will smash the nations like pottery.

In summary, the first proof text establishes that the Messiah possesses the title "My Son" or "God's Son," a title and station superior to that of angels.

> *Or again, "I will be to him a father, and he shall be to me a son"?* (HEBREWS 1:5)

Our writer selects his second passage using a typical rabbinic method. He makes an association between the words "You are my Son, today I have begotten you" in Psalm 2 and the text in 2 Samuel 7:14, "I will be to him a father, and he shall be to me a son." This second text is an important messianic prophecy spoken to King David through the Prophet Nathan:

> When your days are fulfilled and you lie down with your fathers, I will raise up your offspring after you, who shall come from your body, and I will establish his kingdom. He shall build a house for my name, and I will establish the throne of his kingdom forever. I will be to him a father, and he shall be to me a son. (2 Samuel 7:12–14)

We need to take note of four things:

- The "Son of God" title provides the associative link connecting Psalm 2 and 2 Samuel 7.
- The Son of God will be the Seed of David. On a literal level, the prophecy seemingly refers to Solomon, but the apostolic interpretation applies the prophecy to David's ultimate heir, the Messiah son of David.
- The Son of God will possess an eternal throne and eternal kingdom, something Solomon did not attain: "I will establish the throne of his kingdom forever." This verse will be relevant to the argument later.
- The Messiah will build a house (*bayit*) for God's Name. In Biblical Hebrew, the word *bayit* can mean a house, but it can also refer to a household, that is, a family. Here it means both. David wanted to build a Temple, that is, a house for God. God said he would build a house for David, a dynasty—a family for David. The

exhorter understands this "house" to be a household, as God's "family," a "house for my name."

When he brings the firstborn into the world. (HEBREWS 1:6)

As the Son responsible for building a family (a household) for God, Yeshua occupies the position of "firstborn" over that household. God "brings the firstborn into the world" through the incarnation of the Divine Son in the person of Yeshua of Nazareth. The discussion proceeds, using the concept of God's Son building a family (household) for God as a bridge to the subsequent text, a quotation from Deuteronomy 32:43.

He says, "Let all God's angels worship him." (HEBREWS 1:6)

God exalts the Son's status above the angels with the statement, "Let all God's angels worship him" (Hebrews 1:6). Where does our author find this proof text? It comes from the Song of Moses in Deuteronomy 32:43, but you will probably not find it translated that way in your Bible because the writer of the book of Hebrews did not quote from the Hebrew text; he quoted from the Greek Old Testament called the Septuagint (LXX). In the Septuagint, this verse reads differently.

It's not just in the Greek. Scholars found a corresponding Hebrew variant that supports the Greek text in the Dead Sea Scrolls version of Deuteronomy from Qumran. That discovery indicates that the version of the verse found here in Hebrews did appear in some Hebrew Torah scrolls during the days of the apostles. Here is an English rendering of the Greek text:

> Rejoice, ye heavens, with him, and *let all the angels of God worship him;* rejoice ye Gentiles, with his people, and let all the *sons of God* strengthen themselves in him." (Deuteronomy 32:43 LXX)

On a literal level, Moses intended for us to read the term "sons of God" as a parallel term for "angels of God," but the exhorter interprets the "sons of God" in antithesis to the angels who are told to "worship him." In his view, the "sons of God" are the redeemed household of

God, i.e., the community of Yeshua. They are the household (*bayit*) that David's seed will build for God. The superiority of "the Son of God" above the "angels" is established in that the angels are told to "worship him," the third person pronoun "him" being interpreted as the Messiah.

The connection between the three proof texts presented so far is subtle. Notice the progression.

- Text One: Messiah is called God's Son.
- Text Two: The Messiah is called God's Son, and he builds a household, a family for God's name.
- Text Three: The Messiah strengthens the "sons of God" and builds them into a family, but the angels are told to "worship him."

Of the angels he says, "He makes his angels winds, and his ministers a flaming fire." (HEBREWS 1:7)

In our next bridge between proofs, the book of Hebrews takes the phrase "angels of God" in Deuteronomy 32:43 and connects it to "his angels" in Psalm 104. Whereas the Messiah is called the "Son of God," the angels who are told they must worship him are merely messengers and servants:

> Bless the LORD, O my soul! O LORD my God, you are very great! You are clothed with splendor and majesty, covering yourself with light as with a garment, stretching out the heavens like a tent. He lays the beams of his chambers on the waters; he makes the clouds his chariot; he rides on the wings of the wind; he makes his messengers winds, his ministers a flaming fire. (Psalms 104:1–4)

In both Hebrew and Greek, the word that we translate into English as "angel" merely means "messenger." The angels are God's messengers—a station considerably lower than that of members of his household.

Moreover, they are merely winds and flaming fire. In both Hebrew and Greek, the words we translate as "winds" can be translated as "spirits." The angelic hosts are merely spirits, like flames of fire, without corporeal substance.

> *But of the Son he says, "Your throne, O God, is forever and ever, the scepter of uprightness is the scepter of your kingdom. You have loved righteousness and hated wickedness; therefore God, your God, has anointed you with the oil of gladness beyond your companions."* (HEBREWS 1:8-9)

Not content with the proofs presented so far, the exhorter pursues another approach to establish the Messiah's superiority over angels. He leaves off the discussion about the nature of angels and returns to 2 Samuel 7, the text cited earlier, which says, "I will establish the throne of his kingdom forever. I will be his father, and he will be my son." Previously, the argument took its point of departure from the key phrase, "I will be his father, and he will be my son." This time it departs from the key phrase, "I will establish the throne of his kingdom forever." The idea of an eternal throne provides a link to Psalm 45, which also speaks of an eternal throne.

Psalm 45 was King Solomon's wedding song, a psalm from which the sages often derived information about King Messiah and the Messianic Era:

> Your throne, O God, is forever and ever. The scepter of your kingdom is a scepter of uprightness; you have loved righteousness and hated wickedness. Therefore God, your God, has anointed you with the oil of gladness beyond your companions. (Psalm 45:7-8[6-7])

Follow the link from 2 Samuel 7, where it said, "I will establish the throne of his kingdom forever," to Psalm 45, which speaks of Solomon's throne as God's throne: "Your throne, O God, is forever and ever." The apostles found reference to the Messiah in Psalm 45 in the words, "God has anointed you with oil of gladness beyond your companions." Recall that the Messiah is called the LORD's Anointed One in Psalm 2. Here is the critical point the exhorter wanted to make: The eternal throne promised to the seed of David actually belongs to God. It says, "Your throne, O God, is forever."

We should also note that the scepter imagery has reappeared and, in Psalm 45, is specifically associated with Messiah's kingdom. Not inconsequential to the ongoing argument, the Messiah has been anointed with the oil of gladness, a privilege the angels did not receive. Messiah obtained the privilege because he "loved righteousness and hated wickedness," which means he attained God's favor through choosing righteousness, something the angels cannot do because they ordinarily lack free will. Therefore, it says regarding the Messiah, "Your God has anointed you with the oil of gladness beyond your companions" (i.e., beyond the angels).

We observe these three points of connection to the previously cited proof texts:

- The eternal throne promised to David's seed in 2 Samuel 7 belongs to God.
- The Messiah anointed in Psalm 2 is anointed with the oil of gladness.
- The Messiah's scepter from Psalm 2 is a scepter of the kingdom.

> "You, Lord, laid the foundation of the earth in the beginning, and the heavens are the work of your hands; they will perish, but you remain; they will all wear out like a garment, like a robe you will roll them up, like a garment they will be changed. But you are the same, and your years will have no end." (HEBREWS 1:10-12)

From the texts already cited, the argument has established that the Messiah's throne will endure forever. This notion raises a problem expressed in a seemingly contradicting text. The argument cites Psalm 102, which describes how the heavens and the earth "will perish" and "all wear out like a robe, and they will pass away" (Psalm 102:26). If everything is going to perish, be rolled up, and be changed out like a garment, then how can the Messiah possess a throne that will endure forever? How can the kingdom be everlasting if heaven and earth are not? How can his throne last forever if nothing is eternal other than God? The throne of King Messiah will forever endure because it is the throne of God who is "enthroned forever" (Psalm 102:12). The reference to the LORD who sits enthroned forever connects us back to the eternal throne of God that he promises to David's seed in Psalm 45 and 2 Samuel 7.

Psalm 102 is titled "A Prayer of One Afflicted." In apostolic terminology, this psalm speaks of the Messiah, the Suffering Servant. He is the Afflicted One. The psalm depicts God's intention to redeem the exiles and gather them together to Jerusalem so they will praise his name in Zion. He hears "the groans of the prisoners," and he considers how to "set free those who were doomed to die" (Psalm 102:20). But as the psalm describes God's desire to redeem the exiles, the Messiah interrupts and offers a complaint and a petition:

> [The Messiah complains,] He has broken my strength in midcourse; he has shortened my days. "O my God," I [the Messiah] say, "take me not away in the midst of my days—you whose years endure throughout all generations! Of old you laid the foundation of the earth, and the heavens are the work of your hands. They will perish, but you will remain; they will all wear out like a garment. You will change them like a robe, and they will pass away, but you are the same, and your years have no end. The children of your servants shall dwell secure; their offspring shall be established before you." (Psalms 102:23-28, paraphrase)

The Messiah complains that God has "shortened his days" and cut him off in the midst of his years. He asks for life—eternal life, and he extends the petition to include "the children of your servants." Who are these children who are gathered together to worship the LORD, these servants who dwell secure, this seed that is established forever when everything else is rolled up like a garment, changed like a robe, and passes away?

We learn three things from the psalm:

- God's throne is eternal.
- Everything else is temporary.
- Men are prisoners condemned to death.
- The children of God's servants will live in his presence.

The children of God's servants will be established before him. This implies eternal life for those who were condemned to death. Therefore, the household that Messiah builds for God is an eternal one, belonging not to this current age but to the World to Come.

If, on the one hand, the only thing that is going to survive is God's eternal throne where he sits enthroned forever, but, on the other hand, God has also promised that Messiah's throne will last forever, then clearly God must have Messiah sitting with him on his eternal throne. This concept leads us to our next passage, Psalm 110, where God says to the Messiah, "Sit at my right hand."

> *To which of the angels has he ever said, "Sit at my right hand until I make your enemies a footstool for your feet"?* (HEBREWS 1:13)

Psalm 110 depicts the Messiah seated at the right hand of God, that is, at the side of God's throne. This indicates that Messiah's throne is God's throne, which explains how the throne and kingdom of the Messiah can endure forever, past this temporary world and into the eternal World to Come. The scepter that we saw in Psalm 2 and Psalm 45 reappears in Psalm 110 as well, and the Messiah's enemies are made into a footstool, subjugated beneath his feet:

> *A Psalm of David.* [God] says to my [Master]: "Sit at my right hand, until I make your enemies your footstool." [God] sends forth from Zion your mighty scepter. Rule in the midst of your enemies! (Psalm 110:1-2)

The exhorter rhetorically asks his readers, "To which of the angels has God ever made such an offer?"

> *Are they not all ministering spirits sent out to serve for the sake of those who are to inherit salvation?* (HEBREWS 1:14)

Far from attaining such prestige, position, and power, the angels serve merely as "ministering spirits" at God's beck and call. They are assigned to work on behalf of the community of those "who are to inherit salvation." If angels are sent out to serve the followers of Yeshua, clearly, they occupy a position lower than Yeshua. They have no claim to take a seat beside the throne of God, nor does God promise to subjugate their enemies beneath their feet. Rather, they are like the servants in a royal household, not members of the household itself.

This observation leads the exhorter to make some conclusions, which he expresses in Hebrews 2:1-5. Those conclusions will be discussed in the subsequent chapter. For now, we want to continue to follow the chain of linked texts. The prophecy that all things will be placed beneath the feet of the Messiah leads the exhorter to the next text in the chain, a passage from Psalm 8.

> *"What is man, that you are mindful of him, or the son of man, that you care for him? You made him for a little while lower than the angels; you have crowned him with glory and honor, putting everything in subjection under his feet."* (HEBREWS 2:6-8)

The exhorter uses the phrase from Psalm 110, "Until I make your enemies a footstool for your feet," to lead him to Psalm 8, where it speaks of a human being (son of man) exalted above angels when God puts "all things under his feet":

> What is man that you are mindful of him, and the son of man that you care for him? Yet you have made him a little lower than the heavenly beings and crowned him with glory and honor. You have given him dominion over the works of your hands; *you have put all things under his feet.* (Psalm 8:5-7[4-6])

The term "son of man" employed by the psalmist functions as a Hebrew idiom for a human being, but in a messianic context, it takes on greater significance. In the minds of the apostles, the terms "the son of man" and "one like a son of man" functioned as titles for Messiah, and that's how the exhorter employs it here. "What is the Son of Man that you are mindful of him?" He is the Afflicted One lower than the angels, a human being. But God elevated this human being, the Messiah, and made him higher than angels by putting everything, including them, under his feet.

> *Now in putting everything in subjection to him, he
> left nothing outside his control.* (HEBREWS 2:8)

After identifying the "son of man" in Psalm 8 as the Messiah, the exhorter points out that God has exalted him above all creatures and given him dominion over all things made by God's hands. In Psalm 8, the angels are on the level of "the work of your fingers, the moon and the stars, which you have set in place," but the Messiah is made beneath them, in the world of earthly creatures such as "all sheep and oxen ... beasts of the field, the birds of the heavens, and the fish of the sea" (Psalm 8:8-9[7-8]). Although the Messiah is made a part of the lower world, he is exalted above the heavenly spheres when he is given "dominion over the works of your hands." Nothing in existence falls outside of the definition "the works of your hands," not even angels. Therefore, the Messiah holds dominion over even the highest of the angels. Nothing has been left outside of his control.

In this present age, however, we do not yet see the dominion of Messiah over all things (Hebrews 2:8). Instead, as the exhorter has already indicated, it is "the world to come, of which we are speaking" (Hebrews 2:5). Until then, things continue until God fulfills his promise to the Messiah and makes his enemies into a footstool for him and places them beneath his feet.

For the exhorter, the transition from being "made lower than the angels" to being "crowned with glory and honor" took place through the death, resurrection, and ascension of Yeshua, a topic taken up in 2:9-11. That discussion will receive further comment in a subsequent chapter in this book. For now, we want to continue to follow the chain of linked texts to the next passage the exhorter cites.

> *That is why he is not ashamed to call them brothers,
> saying, "I will tell of your name to my brothers; in the midst
> of the congregation I will sing your praise."* (HEBREWS 2:11-12)

Prior to his exaltation, the Messiah was made a human being occupying a station a little lower than the angels. For that reason, he is not ashamed to consider the sons and daughters of men to be his brothers—a concept that leads the exhorter to cite Psalm 22.

The apostolic community considered Psalm 22 a prophetic song of the crucifixion of the Messiah. Its appearance in the gospel passion narratives indicates that the psalm was well-known in the Yeshua community and probably frequently read. The psalm begins with the words, "My God, My God, why have you forsaken me?"—the very words that the Master uttered from the cross before his death. In the psalm, those words anticipate the suffering of the Afflicted One:

> For dogs encompass me; a company of evildoers encircles me; they have pierced my hands and feet—I can count all my bones—they stare and gloat over me; they divide my garments among them, and for my clothing they cast lots. (Psalms 22:17-19[16-18])

When the apostles read Psalm 22, they heard the voice of Messiah speaking prophetically through the Holy Spirit. Here the Messiah refers to the community as his brothers:

> I will tell of your name to my brothers; in the midst of the congregation I will praise you. You who fear the LORD, praise him! All you offspring of Jacob, glorify him, and stand in awe of him, all you offspring of Israel! (Psalm 22:23-24[22-23])

The exhorter identifies the Messiah's brothers "in the midst of the congregation" as "the offspring of Abraham" (Hebrews 2:16), i.e., the Jewish people. Gentile disciples are not really in view in his discussion, but they are in view in Psalm 22. Although the exhorter does not make the point, notice that, according to the same line of interpretation, the Messiah's "brothers" from the "midst of the congregation" would include both God-fearing Gentile believers from the nations ("You who fear the LORD") and the Jewish people ("You offspring of Jacob ... all you offspring of Israel").

Moreover, as the psalm continues, it contradicts the notion that God ever abandoned the Suffering Messiah. Despite appearances or claims to the contrary, God did not abandon him on the cross, nor did he hide his face from him. Instead, when the Messiah cried out, God heard his cry:

> He has not despised or abhorred the affliction of the afflicted, and *he has not hidden his face from him*, but has heard, when he cried to him. (Psalms 22:25[24])

> *And again, "I will put my trust in him."*
> *And again, "Behold, I and the children*
> *God has given me."* (HEBREWS 2:13)

The phrase, "he has not hidden his face from him," provides the missing link to our last proof text, a passage from Isaiah that indicates that, although God has hidden his face from Israel, he has not abandoned the Messiah. Instead, the Messiah waits upon the LORD for his salvation. Even if God has hidden his face from the people, the Messiah intentionally identifies himself with Israel and continues to hope in the LORD:

> I will wait for the LORD, *who is hiding his face from the house of Jacob*, and I will hope in him. Behold, I and the children whom the LORD has given me are signs and portents in Israel from the LORD of hosts, who dwells on Mount Zion. (Isaiah 8:17–18, emphasis mine)

God has heard the cry of Yeshua, the one given over to death. He has given the Messiah a place on his throne. The Messiah brings along with him his younger siblings, the community of Israel, that is, the house he is building for God. They are "the children God has given me."

All this justifies why God made the Messiah as a human being, lower than the angels. Since "the children share in flesh and blood, he himself likewise partook of the same things ... For surely it is not angels that he helps, but he helps the offspring of Abraham" (Hebrews 2:14, 16). In this way, the Messiah builds a household for God, and even now, those who hold fast to him are considered members of his household:

> [The Messiah] is faithful over God's house as a son. And we are his house if indeed we hold fast our confidence and our boasting in our hope. (Hebrews 3:6)

Recapitulation

A quick recap of the chain of linked proof texts yields the following picture. Messiah, the seed of David, is superior to any angel because, even though he was made a human being, lower than the angels, through his suffering, death, and resurrection, he was elevated and given an eternal throne, seated at the right hand of God with the title "Son of God." This is the throne that was promised to the son of David, a throne that will endure after this present world disappears. God will place all created things, even the angels, beneath the feet of the Messiah. His throne and kingdom will endure into the World to Come. Messiah is also building a house for God. Because he has been given a seat on God's throne, he is able to raise his family, the sons of Israel, with him. Because he occupied their station below, he is able to elevate them along with him in his ascension to that place of eternal life where he holds dominion over the future World to Come. Those who place hope in him will be added to the household of God that he is building—that new Temple that will endure forever.

> The words concerning My Servant are told already in the Torah, the Prophets, and the Writings. Where in the Torah? As it says in Exodus 4:22, "Israel is My son, My firstborn." Where in the Prophets? As it says in Isaiah 52:13, "Behold, My servant will prosper," and nearby in Isaiah 42:1, "Behold, My Servant, whom I uphold." Where in the writings? As it says in Psalm 110:1, "The LORD said to my Lord" and in Psalm 2:7, "The LORD, He said to Me, 'You are My Son.'" (*Yalkut Shimoni* II 621)

CHAPTER SIX:
SPOKEN BY ANGELS
(HEBREWS 2:1-8)

If the Torah that came through angels demands respect, how much more so does the message that has come through the Messiah.

Using a web of proof texts, the exhorter has demonstrated that the Son is superior to the angels. After having established his point, the author concludes his argument with a practical application in the form of a word of exhortation:

> Therefore we must pay much closer attention to what we have heard, lest we drift away from it. For since the message declared by angels proved to be reliable, and every transgression or disobedience received a just retribution, how shall we escape if we neglect such a great salvation? (Hebrews 2:1-2)

"The message declared by angels" of which "every violation and disobedience receives its just punishment" is the Torah. The New American Standard Bible better translates the description of the Torah as "the word spoken through angels," which "proved unalterable."

This is another light-to-the-heavy argument. If the Torah spoken through angels proved immutable and must be obeyed, and if the Son is superior to the angels who spoke the Torah, how much more so must we heed what the Son says. That's the main thrust behind the exhorter's long argument to prove that the Son of God is superior to the angels. If Yeshua's authority is higher than that of the angels, his words should be treated as no less weighty than the Torah. This conclusion wraps all the way back to the beginning of the discussion: "In these last days he has spoken to us by his Son" (Hebrews 1:2).

> *Therefore we must pay much closer attention to what we have heard, lest we drift away from it.* (HEBREWS 2:1)

Notice that this light-to-the-heavy argument is persuasive only to a community that is devoted to the Torah's authority. If "the Hebrews" addressed in the book of Hebrews did *not* consider themselves under the authority of the Torah, then the Torah makes an ineffective starting point for the argument. If they dismissed the Torah as obsolete, the conclusion they would have to reach (logically following the *kol v'chomer* in this verse) would be that "just as the Torah is obsolete and irrelevant, how much more so is Yeshua obsolete and irrelevant." This seemingly obvious rhetorical point counters the common interpretation of the book of Hebrews. The standard interpretation assumes that the book was written to non-observant Jewish Christians who had abandoned Judaism for the sake of their Christian convictions but were now in danger of straying back into Jewish Torah observance with its Levitical ceremonies.

> *For since the message declared by angels proved to be [unalterable], and every transgression or disobedience received a just retribution.* (HEBREWS 2:2)

If the Jewish believers considered the Torah as alterable and no longer binding, and if they believed that transgression of the Torah no longer received a just recompense, then the argument falls apart. The exhorter argues, "If the Torah proved unalterable, how much more so does the revelation of the kingdom." But if the Torah is actually mutable, as the conventional interpretation of the book of Hebrews supposes, then the argument collapses.

How does the Bible depict the Jewish believers in the Apostolic Era? The book of Acts paints a careful portrait of them. They were continually in the Temple, devoted to the prayers, the breaking of bread, fellowship, and the Scriptures. There were myriad thousands of Jewish believers, all of them zealous for the Torah. They were devout and observant, taking nazirite vows and even participating in the Temple worship and sacrifices all the way through to the end of the book of Acts. These are all biblical descriptions of "the Hebrews" to whom the letter is addressed. The exhorter reasons *a fortiori* with them because he assumes that they are devoted to the Torah and consider it the authority over their lives.

The message declared by angels. (HEBREWS 2:2)

What exactly does it mean that the Torah was spoken through angels? Internal evidence seems to suggest otherwise. The Torah frequently says, "The LORD spoke to Moses saying," indicating direct communication. Even more strikingly, when Israel stood at the foot of the mountain, all the people heard the voice speaking to them from out of the fire.

However, Hebrews is not alone in attributing some role to angels in the giving of the Torah. Other references to this idea appear in Acts 7 and Galatians 3. Stephen, the Greek-speaking deacon of the assembly, rebukes the court of religious leaders and judges conducting his trial: "You who received the Torah as delivered by angels and did not keep it" (Acts 7:53). In Galatians 3:19, Paul speaks of the Torah as "put in place through angels by [a mediator]." Moses was the mediator between God and Israel, but why does Paul say the Torah was put into effect through angels?

Different Types of Angels

Since "angel" means "messenger," any being God uses to deliver a message can be described as an angel. When we think of angels, we tend to imagine the angels Gabriel or Michael, but those are one specific type of angel—angelic princes, or archangels (*sarim*). The Bible presents several other types of angels as well. In Isaiah 6, we see the *seraphim*, "burning ones," around God's throne: "He makes his servants flames of fire." Ezekiel saw four-faced *cherubim* that carry the throne, and he described them as *chayot*, "living creatures." He also saw *ofanim*, the "wheel angels" on which God's chariot moves. There are also the fallen angelic princes, whose names we will not speak here. Then there are the vast and innumerable *tzava'ot*, the "angelic hosts," the court of God, who are described as rivers of fire emerging from beneath God's throne to carry out his will. They are created for a single purpose, a single message or errand in the administration of the creation.

Yet another type of angel is the representational Angel of the LORD. He speaks directly for God in the first person; he is a physical representation, but he is not really God. He is a projection, a finite metaphysical entity animated by God in time and space so that he can interact with finite mortals. How else was the infinite and uncontainable God, whose essence is described as a consuming fire dwelling in deep darkness, unapproachable and unknowable, supposed to converse with Abraham? He created an angel, a messenger, to speak through, to animate in order to interact with him. The Angel of the LORD is like a garment that God dons to interact with mortals.

The Angel of the LORD

The book of Exodus describes such an encounter when "the angel of the LORD appeared to [Moses] in a flame of fire out of the midst of a bush" (Exodus 3:2). Then "God called to him out of the bush, 'Moses, Moses!'" (Exodus 3:4). Was it the LORD speaking in the bush or was it the Angel of the LORD? It was the LORD speaking through the persona, as it were, of the Angel of the LORD.

In another passage, the LORD tells Moses that he is going to send his angel ahead of Israel to lead them into the land of Canaan:

> Behold, I send an angel before you to guard you on the way and to bring you to the place that I have prepared. Pay careful attention to him and obey his voice; do not rebel against him, for he will not pardon your transgression, for my name is in him. (Exodus 23:20-21)

Who is this angel that will lead Israel and punish rebellion? Who is this angel in whom God's name is placed? It is the Angel of the LORD.

It may be a literary technicality that the expositor exploits to make his point, but technically, the Torah itself was put into effect and spoken through angels, albeit the Angel of the LORD.

Angels at the Giving of the Torah

Two critical verses play a part in the idea of angelic agency behind the giving of the Torah:

> The LORD came from Sinai and dawned from Seir upon us; he shone forth from Mount Paran; he came from the ten thousands of holy ones, with flaming fire at his right hand. (Deuteronomy 33:2)

> The chariots of God are twice ten thousand, thousands upon thousands; the Lord is among them; Sinai is now in the sanctuary. (Psalm 68:17)

Jewish apocalyptic literature also supports the idea of the Torah being given through angels. For example, the apocryphal book of *Jubilees* provides ample examples of this type of angelic agency involved in the giving of the Torah and, for that matter, the rest of God's interactions with Israel.

Rabbinic literature connects the LORD's descent on Mount Sinai and "the chariots of God" with the theophany of Ezekiel 1. For that reason, we read Ezekiel 1 for the haftarah portion on the first day of Shavu'ot. The mention of the LORD's chariots in Habakkuk 3:8 strengthened the passage's association with that holiday. *Pesikta Rabbati* explains, "At the time of the giving of the Torah, twenty-two thousand divine chariots descended with the Almighty, every single one of which resembled Ezekiel's in greatness."

In the days of the apostles, a prestigious, wealthy Jewish philosopher named Philo served as a spokesman for the Greek-speaking Jewish community in Alexandria. He wrote extensively about the Torah and Judaism. His writings give us a glimpse of the theology and interpretations of Hellenistic Judaism during the Apostolic Era. He taught that the Torah was given through angels. He believed that Jacob's dream of a ladder to heaven represented the giving of the Torah when Moses received it from the angels who ascended and descended on Sinai. Philo said that they are called "messengers" because "they report the commandments of the Father to his children" (Philo, *De Somniis* 1:140–144).

> *How shall we escape if we neglect such
> a great salvation?* (HEBREWS 2:2)

The Greek-speaking Jewish writer of the Epistle to the Hebrews says something similar to the sources cited above when he indicates that although in former days God spoke to us through angels, "in these last days he has spoken to us by his Son." The exhorter has the Torah itself in mind because the Torah, in a sense, was spoken through angels. If the Torah, spoken through angels, is steadfast, unchanging, and binding, how much more so is the word spoken through the Son. So be careful that you do not drift away from Yeshua.

The exhorter asks, "Would you consider drifting away from Torah?" Of course not! His readers are faithful men and women of Israel, zealous for the Torah. But if the Son of God occupies a higher station than the angels through whom God gave the Torah, how much less should we drift away from the revelation of Messiah?

Not for the Angels

I will illustrate the idea with a story from the Talmud about the giving of the Torah. The story is told by Yehoshua ben Levi in the form of an explanation of Psalm 8. Although Yehoshua ben Levi lived long after the days of the apostles, the story he tells was probably already in common currency when he told it, and it may date back to the time of the writing of the book of Hebrews:

> When Moses ascended Mount Sinai (and entered into heaven), the ministering angels objected before the Holy One, blessed be He, "Master of the Universe! What business has one born of woman amongst us?"
>
> "He has come to receive the Torah," God answered.
>
> They objected, "Will you really let him have that secret treasure, which you hid away nine-hundred and seventy-four generations before the world was created? Do you really want to give it to flesh and blood? 'What is man that you are mindful of him, and the son of man that you care for him? You have set your glory [the Torah] above the heavens'" (Psalm 8:1, 4).

The Holy One, blessed be He, said to Moses, "You answer them."

Moses replied, "Master of the Universe. I'm afraid to do so lest they incinerate me with the breath of their mouths!"

"Hold on to the Throne of Glory and give them an answer."

Moses said, "Master of the Universe! What does it say in the Torah which you are giving to me? It says, 'I am the LORD your God, who brought you out of the land of Egypt.'" Then he asked the angels, "Did you go down into Egypt? Were you ever enslaved to Pharaoh? Why should you claim the Torah belongs to you?"

Moses said, "Again, what does it say in the Torah? 'You shall have no other gods before me.' Do angels dwell among people that engage in idolatry? It says, 'Remember the Sabbath day, to keep it holy.' Do angels perform work from which they must rest? It says, 'Honor your father and mother.' Do angels have fathers and mothers? It says, 'You shall not murder. You shall not commit adultery. You shall not steal.' Is there jealousy among the angels? Do they have an evil inclination?"

The angels conceded and consented to let the Holy One, blessed be He, give the Torah to Moses. After all, it says (in Psalm 8), "O LORD, our Lord, how majestic is your name in all the earth!" (b.*Shabbat* 88b-9a)

Chasidic Judaism explains that the Torah exists on many different levels. The literal Torah that we read from the scroll and study in this world is merely a manifestation of the divine wisdom that preexisted creation. The Torah, as we know it, speaks in the language of men. It translates, so to speak, the divine wisdom that resides far above and beyond our material existence.

The angels objected to lowering the divine wisdom of the supernal heavenly Torah into the material world where human beings would sully it. Moses argued that the whole purpose of the divine wisdom was to descend into our physical, material world, where God desires to dwell among his people, where there is free will, temptation, decision, and the actual ability to choose yes or no, life or death, to obey or to disobey.

The common rabbinic adage, "the Torah was not given to angels" (b.*Kiddushin* 54a), is based upon the Talmud's explanation of Psalm 8. The Torah was not given to the angels but to human beings who were made "a little lower than the angels." The Torah speaks directly into human society with all of its wrinkles. It speaks in the language of flawed and imperfect human beings to infuse godliness into our world. In the book of Hebrews, the exhorter drives for something similar, employing the same set of proof texts from Psalm 8 to establish that "it was not to angels that God subjected the world to come, of which we are speaking" (Hebrews 2:5).

> *It was declared at first by the Lord, and it was attested to us by those who heard.* (HEBREWS 2:3)

The good-news message of the "great salvation," the weight of which exceeds the Torah "declared by angels," was first declared by the Master Yeshua. He passed it on to the apostles. The message of the great salvation Yeshua taught was the good news of repentance in his name for the forgiveness of sins, whereby the nation might usher in the kingdom, and a person may obtain a share in the World to Come. Yeshua declared that message to the apostles. The apostles, in turn, passed it on to "those who heard," i.e., the second generation of disciples, including the exhorter himself. The exhorter cannot be a first-generation disciple like Peter, nor could he be Paul, who boasted, "I did not receive it from any man, nor was I taught it, but I received it through a revelation of [Yeshua the Messiah]" (Galatians 1:12). Instead, the exhorter must be a second-generation disciple, a disciple of the apostles. Someone like Clement of Rome.

> *While God also bore witness by signs and wonders and various miracles and by gifts of the Holy Spirit distributed according to his will.* (HEBREWS 2:4)

As the apostles transmitted the message of the great salvation they had received from the Master, God himself testified to the veracity of their message by empowering them with "signs and wonders and various miracles." This is like what Paul said to the Corinthians: "The signs of a true apostle were performed among you with utmost patience, with signs and wonders and mighty works" (2 Corinthians 12:12). Likewise, the "gifts of the Holy Spirit distributed according to his will" finds a close parallel in Paul's discourse on such gifts in 1 Corinthians 12.

> *For it was not to angels that God subjected the world to come, of which we are speaking.* (HEBREWS 2:5)

The revelation at Sinai, which came through angels, consisted of this: Moses took the Torah from the realm of angels and gave it to men.

The revelation at Zion, declared by Yeshua, consists of this: Yeshua has taken the World to Come from the realm of angels and delivered it to human beings.

The World to Come is the world of the resurrected. It's not the afterlife (the paradisaic non-corporeal world of souls), nor is it limited to the Messianic Era, which functions merely as its front porch. The World to Come is the new heavens and the new earth where the righteous resurrected will dwell in the presence of God "like angels in heaven" (Matthew 22:30) for eternity:

> For behold, I create new heavens and a new earth, and the former things shall not be remembered or come into mind. (Isaiah 65:17)

By virtue of his resurrection, Yeshua of Nazareth has ascended to the right hand of the throne of glory to take charge over the World to Come, the eternal future of the resurrected righteous. That destiny does not belong to angels, nor is it governed by them.

The exhorter insists that the revelation of the World to Come transcends even the revelation of the Torah that was given at Mount Sinai. The revelation of "the world to come of which we are speaking" is higher than the revelation of the Torah given through angels. The World to Come belongs to the Messiah.

CHAPTER SEVEN:
THE PERFECT
(HEBREWS 2:6–18)

The descent and ascent of the Son of Man in Psalm 8 alludes to the death of the Messiah, his resurrection, and ascension.

In the introductory arguments of the Epistle to the Hebrews, the exhorter establishes that the Son is superior to angels through whom the Torah was given. Therefore, we should heed him as we would heed the Torah. Moreover, the exhorter describes for us the divine nature of the Son, who is the supernal wisdom of God, the radiance of God's glory and the exact imprint of God's nature, the very image of the Holy One, blessed be he. God has subjected all things, including angels and the World to Come, under the authority of the resurrected Son, by virtue of the fact that he became a human being and suffered many trials.

Now in putting everything in subjection to him, he left nothing outside his control. (HEBREWS 2:8)

The exhorter invokes the testimony of Psalm 8 to demonstrate how all things have been subjected to Yeshua's authority:

> It has been testified somewhere, "What is man, that you are mindful of him, or the son of man, that you care for him? You made him for a little while lower than the angels; you

have crowned him with glory and honor, putting everything in subjection under his feet." Now in putting everything in subjection to him, he left nothing outside his control. (Hebrews 2:6–8)

When the apostles read about the elevation of "the son of man" in Psalm 8, they understood the psalm to be speaking about the Messiah, the suffering servant of God of whom Isaiah said, "Behold, my servant shall act wisely; he shall be high and lifted up, and shall be exalted" (Isaiah 52:13). The Servant of the LORD is higher than Abraham, lifted up above Moses, exalted above angels. This Son of Man will rule all nations during the Messianic Era, and to him belongs the World to Come, as has been stated, "It was not to angels that God subjected the world to come, of which we are speaking" (Hebrews 2:5).

The exhorter uses Psalm 8 to teach us that the Son of Man, who was made a little lower than the angels, has been crowned with glory and honor superior to that of angels. Everything has been put beneath his feet, as it says in Psalm 110:1, "Sit at my right hand until I make your enemies a footstool."

This is the theology of the kingdom of heaven, specifically the Messianic Era during which the Davidic Messiah King will subdue the earth and reign in Zion from David's throne. All things will be subject to him, i.e., beneath his feet. The writer of the book of Hebrews says that Yeshua has already acquired this authority because He is already seated at the right hand of glory.

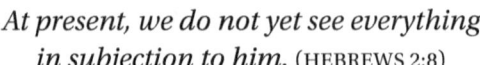

At present, we do not yet see everything in subjection to him. (HEBREWS 2:8)

Everything has been put in subjection to him, leaving nothing outside of his authority. This conviction is difficult to reconcile with the reality of world history. If everything is already subject to Yeshua, why is the world such a mess?

Let me tell you a story to illustrate the point. I try not to listen to the radio, watch television, or even read the newspaper on the Sabbath. I try not to use electronics like computers or smartphones on the Sabbath. The Sabbath is pretty much a twenty-five-hour news blackout for me. So it came to pass that one Friday night in the early 1990s, heavy snow fell, and the city of Saint Paul, Minnesota, declared a snow emergency. During a snow emergency, the streets must be cleared to make room for the snowplows. The city tows away any vehicles left parked on the street and impounds them in a city lot. One of my friends, an Orthodox Jew, happened to be parked on the night-plow side of the street. He could do nothing about it, of course, because, as an Orthodox Jew, he could not start the engine to move his car, and like me, he did not even know that a snow emergency had been declared. Saturday morning, he watched his car being towed away, but he could do nothing to prevent it, nor could he retrieve it until after the Sabbath.

Saturday night, not but moments after he extinguished the havdalah candle, he called me and asked me to drive him to the impound lot. As we got into the car to make the trip, I turned on the radio and quickly flipped through the channels to hear the news. It was the same news: wars and rumors of war, political corruption, crimes, and violence. I explained, "After Sabbath, I always like to check the news to see if the redemption has happened yet." He knew I believed in Yeshua, so he laughed at my optimism. He contended that Yeshua cannot be the Messiah because he failed to bring the redemption. From his perspective, the news proves every day that the redemption has not happened, that the Messianic Era has not yet begun, that we are not yet living in the kingdom, and that Yeshua is not the Messiah. Yet he knew I believed that the Messiah had already come. I suppose it seemed evident to him that if the Messiah had come, we would not be freezing to death, standing in line at the impound lot, paying the seventy-five-dollar fee to get his car back.

Do you see the tension? If all things are subject to the Messiah, and nothing is outside of his authority, what's going on here? Where is the resurrection of the dead, the ingathering of Israel, the defeat of all Israel's enemies, the chaining of the adversary, the subduing of the evil inclination, and the universal peace of the Messianic Age? Why hasn't Zion been rebuilt as an eternal city? Where is the Temple? Why is the wolf still devouring the lamb, and why are the nations still learning war?

Believers believe that the Messiah will accomplish these things at his second coming. But the book of Hebrews states that everything is now in subjection to him; nothing is outside of his authority. When we take a look at the state of the world, we wonder how this can possibly be the case.

The exhorter was neither naïve nor blind. After stating that all things have been placed beneath the feet of Messiah, he added the observation, "At present, we do not yet see everything in subjection to him" (Hebrews 2:8). But according to what we are reading, everything is in place for it to happen. The Son has taken his seat and been given authority. We only wait for what has already been accomplished to be revealed in this current world.

The Absent King

A parable of the Master helps explain the tension:

> A nobleman went into a far country to receive for himself a kingdom and then return. ... But his citizens hated him and sent a delegation after him, saying, "We do not want this man to reign over us." When he returned, having received the kingdom ... he ordered, "As for these enemies of mine, who did not want me to reign over them, bring them here and slaughter them before me." (Luke 19:12–15, 27)

The parable had significant currency in first-century Judea because it more-or-less describes how King Herod the Great and the Herodian kings after him acquired their dominions. In those days, Rome exercised supreme power over the Mediterranean world and beyond. In some cases, they gave local rulers and officials the status of "king" to rule over their subjects. These were merely client kings, loyal to Rome. Before Rome elevated him, Herod was much hated by many of the Jewish people of Judea because, though an outsider, he had inserted himself into a civil war among the Jewish Hasmonean kings. After a severe reversal in his martial fortunes, he fled to Rome, where the Senate granted him the title of King of the Jews. They equipped him with military strength and charged him with subduing the Hasmoneans. This he did—ruthlessly.

Yeshua used the parable to illustrate the coming of the Messiah. It illustrates how a monarch may accede to the throne, with all things put under his feet and under his authority, though he may not have yet suppressed all opposition. In the parable, the nobleman went to a faraway country (Rome) to receive his kingdom. Back at home, the people did not yet know that a new king had been appointed over them. The new king's authority would not be recognized until he had defeated his enemies and put his government in place.

This is the situation in our world today. The Son of Man has gone to a faraway land (the throne of God), where he has been invested with authority and granted a kingdom. Nothing has been left outside of his control. We do not see it because he has not yet returned to put everything in subjection under his feet.

> Now in putting everything in subjection to him, he left nothing outside his control. At present, we do not yet see everything in subjection to him. (Hebrews 2:8)

The Resistance

Let's embellish the Master's parable a bit. Suppose that when Rome appointed the new king, they sent a dispatch with an announcement that the appointment had been made, and we were among those who received the dispatch. The dispatch says, "The Emperor has made so-and-so king over your land. He has absolute power as a monarch over you and all your affairs. Even now, he is seated beside the emperor."

Now we face a decision. Should we cast our loyalty with the newly appointed king or continue to support the pretender currently occupying the throne? If we choose allegiance to the new king, we declare ourselves subjects of his coming kingdom, even though his kingdom has not yet been revealed. We can rightly anticipate that allegiance to the new king will be rewarded when the king comes, and we can anticipate that disloyalty to the official dispatch will likewise be punished.

The pretender continues to occupy the throne and administer the government until the king comes. This puts us in the opposition. If we are loyal to the coming king, we place ourselves in jeopardy from the current ruler. We become the enemy of the powers and authorities currently in place. We become a resistance movement. This is an element of what it means to be in the kingdom before the kingdom comes. To be a disciple of Yeshua means to be *contra mundum*, against the world, the status quo, and the ethos of this present age.

> *We see him who for a little while was made lower than the angels, namely [Yeshua], crowned with glory and honor because of the suffering of death.* (HEBREWS 2:9)

We do not yet see the kingdom, but we see the King; he has already been declared. He became a servant of all, but God raised him to the highest place and made him king over all.

In what sense did the pre-existent Divine Wisdom, the immortal Son, the *Logos* of God, through whom all things were made, become "lower than the angels"? He became lower than the angels in the person of a baby boy born to the house of David. As a human—a mortal being—he became capable of suffering and death like every other human being so that he could suffer and "taste death" for everyone:

> For there is no king that had any other beginning of birth. For all men have one entrance into life, and the like going out. Wherefore I prayed, and understanding was given me: I called upon God, and the spirit of wisdom came to me. I preferred her before sceptres and thrones, and esteemed riches nothing in comparison of her. (*Wisdom of Solomon* 7:5-8, King James Apocrypha)

How did Yeshua attain his high position "crowned with glory and honor" higher than the angels? One might suppose that as the divine *Logos* and Son of God, he inherently possessed the position as a sort of birthright. In that case, he attained kingship because he's Jesus and that's that. He ascended higher than the angels because he always was higher than the angels. However, that's not how the exhorter depicts the ascent of the Messiah. According to the book of Hebrews, Yeshua obtained his exalted status through the merit he achieved "because of the suffering of death."

Our Master taught, "Whoever exalts himself will be humbled, and whoever humbles himself will be exalted" (Matthew 23:12). In apostolic theology, the exaltation of the Messiah is a consequence of his descent. A popular Chasidic axiom teaches the same concept: "What goes down must go up." All of this is to say that, when viewed from the human perspective, Yeshua of Nazareth attained his exalted station of glory on the merit of his obedience. This was God's purpose in him.

> *So that by the grace of God he might taste
> death for everyone.* (HEBREWS 2:9)

To "taste death" is a Hebrew idiom meaning "to die." The divine Son needed to descend below the status of angels and take on flesh and blood because he needed to die, and he needed to die to obtain the resurrection. Through the resurrection, he elevated the human body to the level of angels: "When they rise from the dead, they … are like angels in heaven" (Mark 12:25). The exhorter sees Yeshua as a forerunner who, having obtained that prize, opens the way for others to follow and likewise obtain the resurrection and a share in the World to Come.

> *For it was fitting that [God], for whom and by
> whom all things exist, in bringing many sons to
> glory, should make the founder of their salvation
> perfect through suffering.* (HEBREWS 2:10)

What does it mean that the Messiah was made "perfect through suffering"? Was Yeshua somehow imperfect before he suffered?

The exhorter seems to speak in terms of something attained by Yeshua in his suffering and death, but most believers take it as an article of dogma that Yeshua was already perfect and complete, born flawless from the womb. After all, he was without sin. How perfect can you get?

In the vernacular of the apostles, the term "perfect" often refers to the state of the resurrected body. To enter "the perfect" is to enter the resurrected state and the World to Come. For example, Paul said, "When the perfect comes, the partial will pass away" (1 Corinthians 13:10), and he said he desires to know the power of Messiah's resurrection that "I may attain to the resurrection from the dead. Not that I have already obtained it or have already become perfect, but I press on so that I may lay hold of that for which also I was laid hold of by the Messiah Yeshua" (Philippians 3:10-12 NASB).

Messiah suffered in order to be made *perfect* (Hebrews 2:10), and "being made perfect, he became the source of eternal salvation to all who obey him" (Hebrews 5:9). Whereas the Torah made nothing *perfect* because it appoints mortal men weak in their mortality, the new covenant appoints the Son who was "made *perfect* forever" (Hebrews 7:28). Likewise, the sacrifices can never "make *perfect* those who draw near" (Hebrews 10:1), but through Yeshua, we have a "better hope ... through which we draw near to God" (Hebrews 7:19), in which "the spirits of the righteous [are] made *perfect*" (Hebrews 12:23). Even those great men of faith from previous generations had not attained this *perfection*, but only glimpsed it from afar, so that "apart from us they would not be made *perfect*" (Hebrews 11:40).

Yeshua's suffering perfected him in that through the suffering, he rose from death and took on the imperishable and incorruptible form. He submitted to death only to transcend it. He tasted death, drank it to the dregs, and will never die again. Because of his faithfulness, God raised his mortal body, crowned him, and gave him glory and honor above the angels.

> *For he who sanctifies and those who are sanctified all have one source. That is why he is not ashamed to call them brothers.* (HEBREWS 2:11)

"He who sanctifies" refers to Yeshua, and "those who are sanctified" refers to the redeemed. Yeshua and his people have one source with a common origin in God. Our Master refers to us as his brothers and sisters because the One who declared him the Son has also declared us to be sons and daughters of God. When he appeared to the women who fled from the tomb, he said, "Do not be afraid; go and tell my brothers" (Matthew 28:10). He appeared to Miriam of Magdala and said, "Go to my brothers and say to them, 'I am ascending to my Father and your Father, to my God and your God'" (John 20:17):

> "I will tell of your name to my brothers; in the midst of the congregation I will sing your praise." And again, "I will put my trust in him." And again, "Behold, I and the children God has given me." (Hebrews 2:12-13)

> *Since therefore the children share in flesh and blood, he himself likewise partook of the same things.* (HEBREWS 2:14)

Who are these children of flesh and blood? "Flesh and blood" is simply a Hebrew idiom referring to the physical human body, i.e., a human being. The children who "share in flesh and blood" refers to the redeemed of Israel (and from the nations) who are mentioned in the previous verse, where the Spirit of the Messiah, speaking prophetically through the Prophet Isaiah, says, "Behold, I and the children whom the LORD has given me are signs and portents in Israel from the LORD of hosts, who dwells on Mount Zion" (Isaiah 8:18). They are sons and daughters of the kingdom who have cast their allegiance with Yeshua of Nazareth. The exhorter refers specifically to the people of Israel who share Yeshua's flesh and blood and to whom the Messiah was sent: "He helps the offspring of Abraham" (Hebrews 2:16).

All human beings are "flesh and blood," a poetic way of saying we are corporeal, physical, and mortal creatures. The divine Son "likewise partook of the same things" by putting on mortal raiment. This is the equivalent of the theologically shocking statement in John 1:14: "The Word became flesh and dwelt among us." This is not just a miraculous concept; it is the central miracle around which all other miracles revolve. The incarnation of the Son, the Divine Nature becoming a human, requires the impossible union of creator and creation. It is the vortex of existence that draws all things into it and from which all things emerge.

However, the writer of the book of Hebrews is not pursuing the philosophical implications of this miracle. He has an eye toward a much simpler concept, and that is merely to say that Yeshua of Nazareth lived a mortal human life like the rest of us on planet earth.

> *That through death he might destroy the one who has the power of death, that is, the devil.* (HEBREWS 2:14)

In Judaism, the devil is sometimes depicted as the angel of death. Likewise, in the book of Hebrews, the devil and the angel of death are the same entity. The devil has the power of death because he holds humanity captive to sin, and the law of sin and death states that the wages of sin is death.

The Messiah tasted death to destroy the one with the power of death, which he accomplished by overcoming death through resurrection. Death and the angel of death are among the enemies yet to be defeated and placed beneath his feet. Their defeat is certain and has already begun; it began when Yeshua emerged from the tomb.

An important Pauline passage derives the same message with reference to the same proof texts. Paul and the exhorter seem to have both drawn on a common apostolic interpretation of Psalm 8 about the resurrection:

> But in fact [the Messiah] has been raised from the dead, the firstfruits of those who have fallen asleep. For as by a man came death, by a man has come also the resurrection of the dead. For as in Adam all die, so also in [the Messiah] shall all be made alive. But each in his own order: [The Messiah] the firstfruits, then at his coming those who belong to [the Messiah]. Then comes the end, when he delivers the kingdom to God the Father after destroying every rule and every authority and power. *For he must reign until he has put all his enemies under his feet.* The last enemy to be destroyed is death. (1 Corinthians 15:20–26, emphasis mine)

What was Paul's source for the idea that "he must reign until he has put all his enemies under his feet?" It comes from Psalm 8 and Psalm 110, the same texts the exhorter relies on in Hebrews 2 to teach the same concept. Since death entered the world through a human being, death's defeat could come only through a human being. Death came through a human being's sin; the resurrection comes through a human being's obedience. Since the children share in flesh and blood, "he himself likewise partook of the same things, that through death he might destroy the one who has the power of death, that is, the devil" (Hebrews 2:14). Death is "the last enemy," but we need not fear death, because we have a hope that transcends it—the future resurrection.

> *And deliver all those who through fear of death*
> *were subject to lifelong slavery.* (HEBREWS 2:15)

The fear of death creates a "lifelong slavery" in the conviction that life ends when it ends and goes no further. When a person believes that death is the end and that this world is all there is, he becomes a slave to this world because there is nothing else to live for. "Eat, drink, and enjoy, for tomorrow we die." The person living under "fear of death" is necessarily a slave to materialism and the material world because this is all there is.

The person who believes that death is not the end can escape slavery to this present world. One who believes that this world is the vestibule to the World to Come lives for that future hope, as the exhorter already stated: "Now it was not to angels that God subjected the world to come, of which we are speaking" (Hebrews 2:5). Instead, God subjected the World to Come to the Messiah, placing even it beneath his feet.

> *For surely it is not angels that he helps, but he*
> *helps the offspring of Abraham.* (HEBREWS 2:16)

Hebrews 2:16 reminds us that the epistle is addressed to Jewish people. The exhorter does not use the term "offspring of Abraham" to speak of Abraham's metaphorical children or even the spiritual seed of Abraham through faith, as Paul does in his epistles regarding the Gentile disciples. Instead, the exhorter refers to the literal nation of Israel—the Jewish people. To help the Jewish people, it was necessary for the divine Son to become one of the Jewish people. For that reason, God made him "a little lower than the angels," but now he has been exalted far above them.

The mention of bringing help to "the offspring of Abraham" also reminds us that the epistle's recipients were in danger of losing access to the Temple and the priesthood of Israel. Perhaps they had already been cut off from those resources.

> *Therefore he had to be made like his brothers in every respect, so that he might become a merciful and faithful high priest in the service of God, to make propitiation for the sins of the people.* (HEBREWS 2:17)

To redeem the children and help the sons of Abraham, the divine Son "had to be made like his brothers in every respect." He needed to take on genuine and authentic human mortality, with all its weaknesses and frailties. He did so to be eligible for the role of "a merciful and faithful high priest" who could atone for the sins of the people. With these words, the exhorter introduces the main thrust of his exhortation: Yeshua is a merciful and faithful high priest in the heavenly Temple, where he presents himself in priestly service to atone for sin.

The term "making propitiation for the sins of the people" might allude to the messianic prophecy of Isaiah 53, in which the Servant of the LORD suffers on behalf of the nation of Israel to atone for the sins of the people. The exhorter draws imagery from the Levitical priesthood to depict the Messiah as the priest carrying out an atoning sacrifice on behalf of the nation. The concept of the Messiah's priesthood, only touched upon here, receives significant expansion later in the epistle. At this point, the exhorter merely wants to suggest that the divine Son shared in the flesh and blood of the sons of Abraham to become eligible to serve as priest and make atonement on their behalf. A priest serves as a representative. To represent the sons of Abraham before God, the divine Son also needed to be a son of Abraham. To represent humanity before God, the divine Son also needed to be human.

> *For because he himself has suffered when tempted, he is able to help those who are being tempted.* (HEBREWS 2:18)

Through the human person of Yeshua of Nazareth, the divine Son experienced suffering and testing. The word "tempted" can be read as "enticed to sin" or as "tested." It can also mean "tested by trial and tribulation." The exhorter has the latter meaning in mind in Hebrews 2:18. Yeshua underwent trial and tribulation through his suffering. Therefore, he can empathize with those facing similar trials and tribulations.

This alludes to the epistle's broader context and the concerns of the original readers. The Jewish recipients of the Epistle to the Hebrews suffered disenfranchisement under the priesthood in Jerusalem. They had been alienated from the establishment and, perhaps, already "cut off" by the religious leaders. They seem to have lost access to the Temple and could no longer offer sacrifices, participate in the Temple's ceremonies, or benefit from the atoning ministrations of the priesthood. Moreover, they faced the prospect of persecution from within the Jewish community. To provide the disciples hope in their current circumstances, the exhorter presents Yeshua as a high priest, making atonement for Israel, one who can sympathize with those undergoing trials, suffering, and testing because he himself has already endured the same.

CHAPTER EIGHT:
THE FAMILY OF GOD
(HEBREWS 3:1–6)

> The Messiah occupies the highest position of authority over the family of God, exalted even above the station of Moses.

Disciples in Yeshua's school of students refer to one another with the affectionate and familial address of brother or sister. Yeshua told his disciples, "You are all brothers ... for you have one Father, who is in heaven" (Matthew 23:8-9). In this household of faith, we look to Yeshua as the firstborn and eldest sibling in the family. He also serves as the priest over the family, representing his siblings before the Father.

The exhorter has spent most of the first two chapters of the epistle demonstrating that the divine Son of God temporarily descended to a station lower than the angels to identify with his brethren, Abraham's offspring, so that he might become for them a merciful and faithful high priest in the service of God. Like a Levitical priest employing sacrifices to atone for the nation, the Messiah atones for the sins of the people and delivers them from fear of death. Having also tasted death, he has since entered the perfection of resurrection and obtained an exalted station higher than the angels. He is superior to even to the angelic messengers through whom God gave the Torah; therefore, we should heed his authority no less than that of the Torah. All things will be made subject to him. Because he has prevailed over death through his resurrection, he is able to rescue others from its clutches and elevate them along with him to be reckoned as sons and daughters in the household of God.

> *Therefore, holy brothers, you who share
> in a heavenly calling.* (HEBREWS 3:1)

The author of Hebrews refers to the recipients of his letter as his "holy brothers," a gender-neutral term also meant to include his holy sisters. The Jewish people form a large extended family. It was not unusual for Jewish people in those days to refer to one another with familial language. The early Yeshua followers also adopted fraternal language to refer to fellow disciples. Yeshua himself instituted it when he identified his disciples as "my brother and sister and mother":

> Stretching out his hand toward his disciples, he said, "Here are my mother and my brothers! For whoever does the will of my Father in heaven is my brother and sister and mother." (Matthew 12:49-50)

After the resurrection, Yeshua deliberately heightened that language, broadening his unique relationship with the Father to encompass his disciples. He appeared to the women and said, "Do not be afraid; go and tell my brothers ..." (Matthew 28:10), "Go to my brothers and say to them, 'I am ascending to my Father and your Father, to my God and your God'" (John 20:17). The exhorter states, "That is why he is not ashamed to call them brothers" (Hebrews 2:11).

The disciples of Yeshua "share in a heavenly calling," namely, the call of discipleship to Yeshua and obedience to the good news of the gospel, which called for repentance and allegiance to Yeshua as the Messiah.

> *Consider [Yeshua], the apostle and high
> priest of our confession.* (HEBREWS 3:1)

Why does the writer of the book of Hebrews refer to Yeshua as "the apostle"? The Greek word *apostolos* refers to a messenger sent to act as an agent of another. It corresponds precisely to the Hebrew *shaliach*, a word based on the Hebrew verb *shalach*, "to send." The Master frequently described himself as "the one sent by the Father" and referred to God as "the one who sent me." Variations on that formula appear at least forty times in the Gospel of John. In rabbinic parlance, the term

"Sent One" originally applied to Moses, the one whom God sent to Egypt to speak to Pharaoh and redeem Israel, making it a natural title for the Messiah, the prophet like Moses.

In Judaism, a *shaliach* (sent one/apostle) functioned as a legal representative dispatched to act on behalf of another. The talmudic rule of the *shaliach* stated, "A man's *shaliach* is like the man himself" (m.*Brachot* 5.5), meaning, "A man's *shaliach* has the same legal authority as the man himself" (b.*Nedarim* 72b). The rabbis referred to Moses, Elijah, Elisha, and Ezekiel as God's "sent ones" because they performed deeds and miracles ordinarily performed by God alone.

The term "high priest of our confession" alludes to the argument that will form the main thrust of the book of Hebrews. The exhorter intends to argue that Yeshua now serves as high priest in the heavenly Temple and that the Levitical priesthood on earth is a pale copy of that higher office into which Yeshua has stepped. The argument occupies several of the ensuing chapters, but only here does he refer to him as "high priest of our confession." The term "our confession" occurs again in Hebrews 4:14 and 10:23 with an exhortation to hold fast to it without wavering: "Let us hold fast the confession of our hope" (10:23). This specialized usage indicates that "our confession" must refer to the disciples' faith in Yeshua of Nazareth as the promised Messiah, risen from the dead, through whom comes the redemption, the resurrection, and a share in the World to Come. Yeshua stands at the head of this hope as a high priest stands at the head of the Levitical worship.

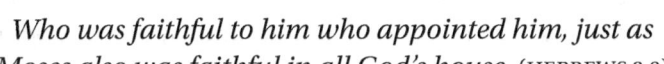

*Who was faithful to him who appointed him, just as
Moses also was faithful in all God's house.* (HEBREWS 3:2)

When Hebrews 3:2 speaks of Moses serving faithfully in "God's house," it uses the term "house" in the sense of a family or a household. Two types of people composed the Roman-era household: slaves and family members. The slaves were the household servants. They belonged to the household; they were part of the family, so to speak, but not part of the inner family. For purposes of comparing the station of Moses with that of the Messiah, the exhorter suggests that Moses served in the household of God on the level of a faithful servant. This idea comes from Numbers 12, where the LORD says, "My servant Moses. He is faithful in all my house":

He said, "Hear my words: If there is a prophet among you, I the LORD make myself known to him in a vision; I speak with him in a dream. Not so with *my servant Moses. He is faithful in all my house.* With him I speak mouth to mouth, clearly, and not in riddles, and he beholds the form of the LORD. Why then were you not afraid to speak against my servant Moses?" (Numbers 12:6-8, emphasis mine)

The sages cite this passage to prove that Moses received a level of prophetic revelation unsurpassed by any other prophet. The other prophets see their prophetic vision the way a man sees his reflection when looking into a tarnished, unpolished mirror, but Moses can be compared to a man looking into a polished mirror. The other prophets saw their visions like a man looking at an image reflected through nine lenses, but Moses perceived prophetic visions clearly through a single lens.

An interesting subtlety in the argument alludes to a text that was already quoted, where the LORD said to David through the Prophet Nathan, "Would you build me a *house* to dwell in?" (2 Samuel 7:5). In that passage, and its parallel in 1 Chronicles 17, the LORD promises to build a *house* for David by building a dynasty through one of his sons. The exhorter seems to employ 1 Chronicles 17:14, where the LORD promises David, "I will establish him in my house." The Hebrew version of the text reads "*V'ha'amadtihu*," which literally means, "I will cause him to stand" or "I will establish him." The Greek Septuagint version uses the word *pistono*, which means "faithful" but can also mean "appointed." The expositor seems to have both versions in view when he refers to Yeshua as one "faithful" and "appointed" within the house of God.

> *For [Yeshua] has been counted worthy of more glory than Moses—as much more glory as the builder of a house has more honor than the house itself.* (HEBREWS 3:3)

The exhorter combines Numbers 12:6-7 and 2 Samuel 7:13-14 by connecting the *house* in the former with the *house* in the latter. The *house* in Numbers 12 is the household of God in which Moses serves as a faithful servant. The *house* in 1 Samuel 7 pertains both to the Temple and the Davidic dynasty that the Son of David will build.

Moses is a servant in the house. He is the greatest of all the servants and the chief steward, but he is not the heir, the son, or the builder of the house. The promised son of David is called a Son of God, as it says, "I will be to him a father, and he shall be to me a son" (2 Samuel 7:14) and "You are my Son, today I have begotten you" (Psalm 2:7, Cf. Hebrews 1:5).

More than just a household servant, Yeshua is called the "builder of the house" because God promised David that he would build him a house through his son. "He shall build a house for my name, and I will establish the throne of his kingdom forever. I will be to him a father, and he shall be to me a son" (2 Samuel 7:13-14). Since the Messiah fulfills the Davidic prophecy, the Messiah is responsible for building the *house* promised to David.

For every house is built by someone, but the builder of all things is God. (HEBREWS 3:4)

"Unless the LORD builds the house, those who build it labor in vain" (Psalm 127:1). Even though God is the builder of all things, he works through an agent to construct what is made. Although he promised to build a house for David, he chose to do so through David's son, the Messiah. In the prophecy to David, the LORD said that David's son "will build my house." On a literal level, this refers to Solomon's construction of the Temple. However, the exhorter uses the prophecy to speak of the household of God, i.e., the community of the redeemed who hold fast to their confidence and hope (Hebrews 3:6). The construction of this house fulfills the promise God made to David: "The LORD declares to you that the LORD will make you a house" (2 Samuel 7:11). As the builder of all things, God constructs the house he promised to David, but he does so through Yeshua.

> *Now Moses was faithful in all God's house*
> *as a servant, to testify to the things that*
> *were to be spoken later.* (HEBREWS 3:5)

Moses did not build the household. He merely served within the household as a faithful servant. He testified about the future redemption (Deuteronomy 30), predicting "things that were to be spoken later." He predicted a future redemption but did not indicate how it would take place or by whose hands it would be accomplished. Those things were "spoken later" when made clear by the message of Yeshua and the apostles.

> *But [Messiah] is faithful over God's*
> *house as a son.* (HEBREWS 3:6)

Moses attained the highest honor possible, rising to the level of chief servant over the household of God, but even the highest slave occupies a lower station than the son of the household. Since Numbers 12 identifies Moses as the "servant" in God's house but 2 Samuel 7 identifies the Davidic heir as the "son" of the household who builds the house, the Messiah holds the higher honor. Therefore, the word of Messiah and allegiance to him ranks even above the authority of the Torah and allegiance to Moses. This should not be understood to mean that Yeshua's authority in any way replaces or discards the authority of the Torah (as is commonly taught in replacement theology). The exhorter does not intend to introduce any dichotomy between the servant of the household and the son of the household. Instead, he predicates the rhetorical punch of his argument on the ongoing authority of Moses and the Torah. The idea is not one of replacement or supersession.

> *And we are his house if indeed we hold fast our*
> *confidence and our boasting in our hope.* (HEBREWS 3:6)

The exhorter conflates the prophecy about Solomon building the Temple as a house for God with the promise that God will establish a household (dynasty) for King David through his heir. Without supplanting either the literal Temple or the literal dynasty of David, the exhorter draws a new significance from the prophecies and applies them to the community of Yeshua's disciples in the midst of Israel.

God's "house" is the Temple. When the exhorter says, "We are his house," he may be invoking the apostolic concept of the community of Yeshua forming a living Temple—not as a literal building but as a household and family. In this sense, the disciples of Yeshua are elevated to the status of sons and daughters of one Father in the "family of God."

The household of God that the Messiah has built comprises those who hold fast to their confidence in him and continue to boast in their hope in the World to Come. This "confidence" consists of the conviction that Yeshua is the divine Son of God and Davidic heir raised from the dead to accomplish the messianic redemption. The "hope" consists of the expectation of attaining the resurrection of the dead, the kingdom, and a share in the World to Come by virtue of allegiance to Yeshua and obedience to his message.

More Worthy of Honor

Let's recapitulate the argument. How do we know that the Messiah will be more worthy of honor than Moses? The Holy One, blessed be he, spoke of Moses, saying, "My servant Moses is faithful in all my house," but he spoke regarding the Son of David, saying, "He shall build a house for me, and I will establish his throne forever. I will be to him a father, and he shall be to me a son." Which of these is the greater, the chief servant of the household or the son over the household?

This discussion evokes the midrash from *Yalkut Shimoni* that speaks of Messiah "high and lifted up greatly," as "lifted above Moses," and as "more exalted than the ministering angels." Previous chapters in the epistle established the Messiah's superiority to angels; chapter three lifts him above Moses.

Moses represents the authority of the Torah. According to the conventional interpretation put forward in support of replacement theology, the Messiah's exaltation above Moses becomes yet another opportunity to overturn the Torah by setting it in opposition to Yeshua and the New Testament. The reasoning goes like this: "The Torah was pretty good, but it was just the word of the servant. Now the Son comes.

A son is not subject to a servant. He cancels the Torah, and releases us from its authority."

That's not the intention of the passage. Instead, the exhorter follows the same argument he advanced in the previous chapter regarding the angels and the Torah. He argued *a priori* that if the Torah put in place by angels holds authority, the message given through the Son (who is higher than angels) has much more authority. The argument here is structurally identical. If Moses had authority as the chief servant over God's household, how much more so does the heir, the Son of that household, wield authority?

> For since the message declared by angels [i.e., the Torah] proved to be [unalterable,] and every transgression or disobedience received a just retribution, how shall we escape if we neglect such a great salvation? (Hebrews 2:2-3)

The exhorter only means to warn his readers against falling away from Yeshua and the revelation received from him. He warns them not to diminish Yeshua or consider him any less essential in their relationship with God than the Torah of Moses.

Rather than doing away with the Torah or placing Messiah in antithesis to the authority of the Torah, the Messiah stands taller than Mount Sinai because he stands atop it.

CHAPTER NINE:
ENTER MY REST
(HEBREWS 3:7–4:9)

The story of the generation of Moses that perished in the wilderness provides a cautionary tale about the potential of forfeiting the kingdom and the World to Come.

Synagogues recite Psalm 95 every Friday night as part of the *Kabbalat Shabbat* service to welcome the Sabbath. The Sabbath liturgy selects this psalm because it refers to God's "rest," which can be understood as the Sabbath day, the day that God rested from creating the heavens and the earth. The psalm concludes with a warning not to be hard-hearted like the generation of Moses that tested God in the wilderness and refused to enter the promised land:

> Today, if you hear his voice, do not harden your hearts, as at Meribah, as on the day at Massah in the wilderness, when your fathers put me to the test and put me to the proof, though they had seen my work. For forty years I loathed that generation and said, "They are a people who go astray in their heart, and they have not known my ways." Therefore I swore in my wrath, "They shall not enter my rest." (Psalms 95:7-11)

The exhorter quotes this psalm in Hebrews 3 as part of a broader warning against failing to heed Yeshua, but the argument is difficult to follow unless we understand how he employs the text. A key to unlocking the passage involves the meaning of the word "rest." What does the psalm mean when it declares that the generation of Moses did not enter God's rest? Three equally valid interpretations of the verse all have some relevance to making sense of Hebrews 3 and 4.

Rest Means Shabbat

What does "They shall not enter my rest" mean? Perhaps it means that the children of Israel did not enter into the Sabbath. The Hebrew word *Shabbat* comes from a verb (*shavat*) that means "to cease" or "to rest." The Torah says, "On the seventh day God finished his work that he had done, and he rested (*shavat*)" (Genesis 2:2). That's why the seventh day is called Shabbat—because it is a day of *shavat*, a day of ceasing and resting from creating. But the Hebrew of Psalm 95:7 uses a different word for "rest." It uses the Hebrew word *menuchah*, another term often associated with the Sabbath. The Hebrew text of Psalm 95 reads, "They shall not enter my *menuchah*." The verbal form of this word, *nuach*, also means "to rest." The Bible uses the term to describe how God rested on the seventh day:

> For in six days the LORD made heaven and earth, the sea, and all that is in them, and rested (*nuach*) on the seventh day. Therefore the LORD blessed the Sabbath day and made it holy. (Exodus 20:11)

On the strength of this association, one could translate Psalm 95:11 to read, "They shall not enter my Sabbath rest." This explains why the synagogue liturgy employs this psalm in the liturgy for welcoming the Sabbath.

The sages also recognized that the psalm has a further, albeit subtle, connection to the Sabbath in the words, "Today, if you hear his voice." The Hebrew word for "today (*haYom*)" can also be understood as "the day," and when singled out from the other days of the week, "the day" refers to God's holy day. "This is *the day* the LORD has made, let us rejoice and be glad in it" (Psalm 118). In Exodus 16, Moses explicitly says that *today* is the Sabbath, and he refers to the Sabbath as "*haYom*" three times:

> Moses said, "Eat it today (*haYom*), for today (*haYom*) is a Sabbath to the LORD; today (*haYom*) you will not find it in

the field. Six days you shall gather it, but on the seventh day, which is a Sabbath, there will be none. (Exodus 16:25-26)

In summary, the sages recognized two references to the Sabbath in Psalm 95:

- *HaYom* if you hear his voice = The Sabbath if you hear his voice.
- They shall not enter my *menuchah* = They shall not enter my Sabbath rest.

According to this interpretation of the psalm, the generation of Israel in the wilderness forfeited the right to enter God's Sabbath rest, which symbolizes the Messianic Era and life in the World to Come. The sages taught that every Sabbath is a foretaste of the Messianic Era, and they referred to the World to Come as the day that is entirely Sabbath.

Rest Means the Promised Land

Here's another nuance behind the words, "They shall not enter my rest." The psalmist speaks about how the generation of Moses perished in the wilderness over the course of forty years. On a literal level, the *menuchah* that they failed to enter was the promised land, the land of Israel.

The Torah tells the story of how Moses sent out twelve spies to reconnoiter the land of Canaan. The mission took forty days, and at its conclusion the children of Israel were supposed to enter the promised land and conquer it. If they had followed Moses into Canaan, they would have obtained the inheritance God promised to Abraham, Isaac, and Jacob. At that moment, the entire generation stood poised on the edge of seeing the fulfillment of those promises. Entering the land at that moment with Moses would have been the culminating pinnacle of the story of their redemption. Instead, they refused to enter God's land of "rest." Their lack of faith resulted in forfeiture of the goal. The LORD regarded it to be a grievous sin.

On the ninth day of the fifth month (the biblical month of Av), the spies returned and gave a bad report. The children of Israel accepted their counsel and refused to enter the land. Judaism still mourns over that tragic mistake annually. The Jewish people observe the anniversary of the incident with a day of fasting and mourning. This same day also became the anniversary of the exile from the promised land. In 586 BCE, the Babylonians destroyed Jerusalem and demolished the Temple on the ninth day of Av—the same day that the generation of Moses refused to enter the land. Seventy years later, some of the exiles returned and rebuilt Jerusalem and the Temple. In the days of the apostles, the Romans destroyed the Temple again on the very same day—the ninth day of the fifth month. The Roman destruction began a second exile that has persisted into the modern era. The synchronicity of these events goes beyond mere coincidence.

When the generation of Moses sinned by refusing to enter the land, the LORD made a solemn oath, banning the generation that left Egypt from entering the land of Canaan:

> But truly, as I live, and as all the earth shall be filled with the glory of the LORD, none of the men who have seen my glory and my signs that I did in Egypt and in the wilderness, and yet have put me to the test these ten times and have not obeyed my voice, shall see the land that I swore to give to their fathers. And none of those who despised me shall see it. (Numbers 14:21-23)

Psalm 95 alludes to the contents of the oath. Ordinarily, a person swearing an oath makes a declaration invoking a deity: "As God lives, I will do such and such." Who does God swear by if he wants to take an oath? "Since he had no one greater by whom to swear, he swore by himself" (Hebrews 6:13):

> As I live, declares the LORD ... According to the number of the days in which you spied out the land, forty days, a year for each day, you shall bear your iniquity forty years, and you shall know my displeasure. I, the LORD, have spoken. Surely this will I do to all this wicked congregation who are gathered together against me: in this wilderness they shall come to a full end, and there they shall die. (Numbers 14:28, 34-35)

Because they refused to heed God's voice, they spent forty years in the wilderness, banned from entering the promised land of rest:

> Your fathers put me to the test and put me to the proof, though they had seen my work. For forty years I loathed that generation and said, "They are a people who go astray

in their heart, and they have not known my ways." Therefore I swore in my wrath, "They shall not enter my *menuchah*." (Psalms 95:9-11)

The word *menuchah* can refer to a time of peaceful rest, but it can also refer to a resting place. Psalm 23, for example, says, "He leads me beside still waters," "*al mei m'nuchot*," "beside waters of resting places." In the synagogue, when the Torah is returned to the ark at the end of the Torah service, the congregation says, "Arise, O LORD, and go to your resting place" (Psalm 132:8). In Isaiah 66:1, the LORD rhetorically asks, "Where is a place that I may rest?" That is, "Where is the place of my *menuchah*?" On the strength of such associations, Psalm 95:11 could mean, "They shall not enter my resting place, the land of Israel."

Rest Means the Kingdom and the World to Come

So far, we have learned two possible interpretations of the LORD's *menuchah* in Psalm 95:11:

- They shall not enter my Sabbath rest.
- They shall not enter my promised land.

The sages offered a third interpretation to explain the meaning behind the words, "They shall not enter my rest." Rabbi Akiva taught that the type of "rest" in question referred to a portion in the World to Come:

> The generation of the wilderness has no portion in the world to come, as it is written: For forty years I loathed that generation and said, "They are a people who go astray in their heart, and they have not known my ways." Therefore I swore in my wrath, "They shall not enter my rest." (b.*Sanhedrin* 110b)

According to Rabbi Akiva's interpretation, the *menuchah* of God is the resurrection of the dead. The generation in the wilderness forfeited the resurrection and will not have access to the Messianic Era or the World to Come.

Does this mean that the generation in the wilderness is damned? Not necessarily. Rabbi Akiva isn't the judge over final destinies. The Talmud presents Akiva's view as just one opinion and not a popular one, either. Rabbi Shimon bar Manasya countered, "They will enter the age to come, as it said [in Isaiah 35:10], 'And the ransomed of the LORD shall return and come to Zion with singing.'" Rabbi Yochanan also objected to Akiva's opinion. He complained, "Rabbi Akiva abandoned his love!" Yochanan goes on to offer additional proof texts that the generation in the wilderness will enter the promised land to participate in the Messianic Era at the time of the final redemption. Other opinions claim that in the final redemption, when the resurrection comes, Moses will also arise with his generation and finally enjoy the privilege of leading them into the promised land.

Despite objections from his colleagues, Akiva's opinion that the LORD's *menuchah* refers to final destinies in the Messianic Era and the World to Come brings our total number of potential interpretations up to three:

- They shall not enter my Sabbath rest.
- They shall not enter my promised land.
- They shall not enter my kingdom/the World to Come.

Which one of these three possible interpretations does the exhorter have in mind when he quotes Psalm 95:11 in Hebrews 3? Does he understand "My rest" as the Sabbath rest, the promised land, or the reward of the World to Come?

Therefore, as the Holy Spirit says. (HEBREWS 3:7)

By invoking the Holy Spirit as the author of Psalm 95, the exhorter implies that the psalm has prophetic significance for his readers. According to the Jewish interpretation of the Psalms, David wrote and sang all of his psalms under the inspiration of the Holy Spirit. Legend says that David would set his harp in his window before going to bed. At midnight, a holy wind (the Holy Spirit) would blow through its strings, setting them to vibrate. The sound of the music woke David every night, and he spent the remainder of the night in Torah study. The same Holy Spirit inspired the words of his psalms. David's heart was like the strings of the harp upon which the Spirit of God played.

The apostolic community believed that the Holy Spirit inspired the psalms as prophetic texts full of hints and clues about the Messiah and his generation. The exhorter detects that type of prophetic foreshadowing at work in Psalm 95. He sees direct parallels between the generation of Moses that died in the wilderness and the generation of the apostles:

Generation of Moses	Generation of Messiah
Redemption from Egypt	Final redemption
Wicked generation	Wicked generation
Poised to enter the promised land	Poised to enter the kingdom, Messianic Era
They lost their opportunity	The potential to lose the opportunity is here
They did not heed "Today"	In danger of not heeding "Today"

Take care, brothers, lest there be in any of you an evil, unbelieving heart, leading you to fall away from the living God. (HEBREWS 3:12)

The exhorter writes to a community of Jewish believers in the last decade before the destruction of the Temple. That disillusioned and weary community has been holding onto the hope of Yeshua's return for more than three decades already. After three decades of waiting, the community has begun to wonder if he really is coming back. As the community faces increased persecution, mounting social pressure, and the cynicism resulting from more than thirty years of hope deferred, they are in danger of drifting away from their allegiance to Yeshua and his message. The exhorter warns his readers not to give any place to fellow community members harboring "an evil, unbelieving heart" because their cynicism will surely compromise the faith of the others. Like the ten wicked spies that disheartened the entire nation, doubters and scoffers might cause the whole community "to fall away from the living God."

> *But exhort one another every day, as long as it is called "today," that none of you may be hardened by the deceitfulness of sin.* (HEBREWS 3:13)

Rather than listen to the discouraging words of those who harbored "an evil, unbelieving heart," the disciples should exhort one another daily to hold fast to their "original confidence" in Messiah. They should encourage one another "every day, as long as it is called 'today.'" This rhetorical flourish is similar to the advice of Rabbi Eliezer, who told his disciples that a person should "repent one day before your death":

> We learnt elsewhere, R. Eliezer said, "Repent one day before your death." His disciples asked him, "Does then one know on what day he will die?" "Then all the more reason that he repent today," he replied, "lest he die tomorrow, and thus his whole life is spent in repentance." (b.*Shabbat* 153a)

Another story from rabbinic lore uses the same text from Psalm 95 to illustrate that a person should repent every day. In the story, Rabbi Yehoshua ben Levi is privileged to meet the Messiah. He asks him, "When will you come to redeem Israel?" The Messiah replies, "Today." Later, Rabbi Yehoshua ben Levi encounters Elijah and complains that the Messiah deceived him. "He said, 'Today,' but he did not come that day." Elijah explained, "You did not understand him. He meant, 'Today—if you hear his voice.'" The Messiah's answer alluded to Psalm 95. That is to say, the Messiah will not come until "the day" that the nation of Israel hears God's voice and repents (b.*Sanhedrin* 98a).

On this basis, the Talmud teaches that "today" means the day when Israel repents. To hear God's voice means to obey him. It means, "today if you will obey me":

> If all Israel would repent even for one day, the son of David would immediately arrive, as this verse attests: "Even today, if we but heed his voice." ... Scripture refers to the Sabbath as "Today," ... and the Psalmist assures Israel, "Even today the Messiah will come, if we but heed his voice." (y.*Ta'anit* 1:1)

It's worth adding that in the apocalyptic worldview of first-century Jews, the term *haYom* ("the day") could also be used as a shorthand allusion to the eschatological "day of the LORD" when the Messiah comes to establish the kingdom, reward the righteous, and punish the wicked. Moreover, "the day" of Messiah's coming is compared to the Sabbath rest. As explained above, the Hebrew word for today, *haYom* ("the day"), can be used idiomatically to indicate the Sabbath, alluding to the Sabbath rest of the Messianic Era.

For we have come to share in [Messiah], if indeed we hold our original confidence firm to the end. (HEBREWS 3:14)

The exhorter warns his readers not to let go of their "original confidence" in Yeshua: his messiahship and the coming redemption by his hand. Those who hold fast to that confidence have a "share in [Messiah]"; that is to say, they will experience the messianic redemption and receive a share in the World to Come. But that share in Messiah and the World to Come is contingent upon their remaining steadfast in their faith and confession of Yeshua.

As it is said, "Today, if you hear his voice, do not harden your hearts as in the rebellion." (HEBREWS 3:15)

Employing the words of Psalm 95, the exhorter reminds his readers that they have heard the voice of God through Yeshua: "In these last days he has spoken to us by his Son, whom he appointed the heir of all things" (Hebrews 1:2). Disloyalty to Yeshua is equivalent to disobedience to God. If they do not maintain their allegiance to Yeshua, they will be no different from the generation in the wilderness who hardened their hearts and refused to enter the promised land. They will forfeit their opportunity to enter into God's rest.

For who were those who heard and yet rebelled? Was it not all those who left Egypt led by Moses? (HEBREWS 3:16)

Carrying the analogy between his generation and the generation of Moses a step further, the exhorter reminds his readers that those who perished were the same people Moses led out of Egypt. Although he had saved them from Egypt, it did not benefit them in the end because they did not remain faithful to Moses. When they rebelled against him, they forfeited the promised land. Likewise, the disciples are in danger of forfeiting their share in the redemption and the World to Come if they rebel against Yeshua.

> *And with whom was he provoked for forty years? Was it not with those who sinned, whose bodies fell in the wilderness?* (HEBREWS 3:17)

The exhorter wrote this exhortation in the decade prior to the outbreak of the Jewish Revolt. The exhorter did not foreknow the events about to transpire. Like the apostles before him, he hoped that if the nation repented under the authority of Yeshua for the forgiveness of sins, the Messiah would come to establish the kingdom, but he warns his readers about another possibility: redemption could be forestalled. Their generation could fail to enter God's "rest," just as the generation of Moses had failed to enter Canaan. He warns them they might make the same mistake as the generation with whom God was angry for forty years.

> *And to whom did he swear that they would not enter his rest, but to those who were disobedient?* (HEBREWS 3:18)

More than three decades had already passed since Yeshua proclaimed that the kingdom of heaven was at hand. The exhorter knows that the Jewish people have, by and large, thus far failed to respond and enter the kingdom, just as the generation of Moses failed to enter the promised land. From the exhorter's perspective, it is natural to make a direct correlation between what happened in the year the Master died and the rejection of the land. Since then, nearly an entire generation has already elapsed. The deadline for the generation to enter the "rest" looms ahead. After all, Yeshua said, "This generation will not pass away until these things are fulfilled." In the story of the ten spies, the generation endured forty years. If the exhorter made a similar correlation regarding the years that had elapsed since the death and resurrection of Yeshua, he knows that the remaining time for the generation to respond to the message grows short.

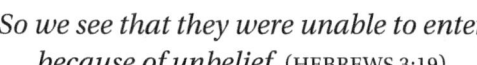

So we see that they were unable to enter because of unbelief. (HEBREWS 3:19)

Allow me to reiterate the correlations. Nearly forty years before the writing of the epistle, Yeshua proclaimed to his generation, "Repent, the kingdom of heaven is at hand." The religious leadership of Judea, followed by a majority of Israel, refused Yeshua's offer of the kingdom. His call for repentance fell on deaf ears. His generation forfeited the kingdom. Like the generation of Moses who refused to enter the land, "they were unable to enter [the kingdom] because of unbelief."

At the time of the writing of the Epistle to the Hebrews, however, nearly forty years since that time had already elapsed, and a second generation stood poised on the edge of the redemption. However, their entrance into the kingdom was no more guaranteed than it had been for their fathers' generation. If they failed to repent, they would forfeit the opportunity just as the previous generation had done forty years earlier.

The math checked out. Forty years after Yeshua's death, on the fast of Av (the ninth day of the fifth month)—the anniversary of the day that the generation of Moses disobeyed and rejected the promised land—the Romans destroyed the Temple, and the second exile began.

The rest of Epistle to the Hebrews contains encouragement and exhortation for surviving the exile and for reaching the redemption. Although we have argued that the exhorter composed the epistle before the beginning of the Jewish war with Rome and well before the destruction of the Temple, it seems as if the entire epistle prophetically prepares the reader for those events. "Before the Holy One, blessed be He, inflicts the wound, He prepares the remedy" (b.*Megillah* 13b). The word of consolation and exhortation of the Epistle to the Hebrews seems to bear prophetic significance. It somehow anticipated the destruction of the Temple and prepared the disciples of Yeshua for the long exile to come, during which Israel has had no priesthood and no Temple:

> For the children of Israel shall dwell many days without king or prince, without sacrifice or pillar, without ephod. (Hosea 3:4)

> *Therefore, while the promise of entering his rest still stands, let us fear lest any of you should seem to have failed to reach it.* (HEBREWS 4:1)

The "promise of entering his rest" that "still stands" refers to the potential redemption. The messianic redemption encompasses all three possible interpretations of *menuchah* explained above. The redemption entails the ingathering of Israel's exiles to the promised land, the spiritualized "Sabbath rest" of the Messianic Era, and the reward of a share in the World to Come through resurrection. However, the disciples to whom the epistle was addressed risked forfeiting all three: possession of the land of Israel, entrance into the day (*haYom*) that is entirely Sabbath, and a share in the World to Come, if they did not hold fast to their confidence in Yeshua and failed to heed him.

> *For good news came to us just as to them.* (HEBREWS 4:2)

What was the "good news" that came to the children of Israel in the wilderness? The exhorter does not mean that the generation in the wilderness received a special revelation about faith in Yeshua as the Messiah. The writer has already explained the good news to be "the promise of entering his rest," which, in the context of the generation of Moses, referred to entering the promised land. He alludes specifically to the good report on the land of Israel offered by Joshua and Caleb as they urged the children of Israel to go up and take possession of Canaan:

> The land, which we passed through to spy it out, is an exceedingly good land. (Numbers 14:7)

> *But the message they heard did not benefit them, because they were not united by faith with those who listened.* (HEBREWS 4:2)

Joshua and Caleb's perspective differed from that of the other ten spies because they heeded God's promises to the patriarchs. They believed that God would give the land to the Jewish people as he promised the forefathers. Caleb said, "Let us go up at once and occupy it, for we are well able to overcome it (Numbers 13:30). Joshua and Caleb believed in the promises of God.

The generation of Moses forfeited the benefit they might have received from the good news proclaimed by Joshua and Caleb "because they were not united by faith" with them. The exhorter wants his readers to think of Yeshua and the apostles as the Caleb and Joshua of their generation. He urges them to unite themselves by faith with the apostolic message about the redemption, the kingdom, and the World to Come.

For we who have believed enter that rest, as he has said, "As I swore in my wrath, 'They shall not enter my rest.'" (HEBREWS 4:3)

The disciples of Yeshua who have believed the good report Yeshua and the apostles brought to them are eligible to "enter that rest," that is, to enter the kingdom and the World to Come. Those who reject the message as the generation of Moses rejected the good report of Caleb and Joshua will not enter the redemption.

Although his works were finished from the foundation of the world. For he has somewhere spoken of the seventh day in this way: "And God rested on the seventh day from all his works." And again in this passage he said, "They shall not enter my rest." (HEBREWS 4:3-5)

The expositor transitions back to the Sabbath day metaphor, juxtaposing Genesis 2:2 and Psalm 95. After six days of creation, God rested, not because he suffered from exhaustion and needed recuperation but because the work of creation was finished and complete. He did not go back to the work of creating the next day; therefore, "his rest remains." The expositor takes this perfected and completed state of God's rest as a symbol of the perfect and unchanging World to Come, which remains a future reward for the people of God.

> *Since therefore it remains for some to enter it, and those who formerly received the good news failed to enter because of disobedience.* (HEBREWS 4:6)

Not everyone will enter the kingdom and the World to Come. Just as those who received the good report about the promised land from Joshua and Caleb failed to benefit from it because of their disobedience, likewise, the disciples of Yeshua might fail to enter the kingdom and World to Come if they turn away from the good-news message proclaimed by Yeshua and his disciples.

> *Again he appoints a certain day, "Today," saying through David so long afterward, in the words already quoted, "Today, if you hear his voice, do not harden your hearts."* (HEBREWS 4:7)

When King David wrote Psalm 95, the generation of Moses that had failed to enter the promised land was long dead. Why then did David declare in the present tense, "Today, if you hear his voice, do not harden your hearts"? This declaration indicates that there remains yet another type of "rest" that awaits the people of God if they will heed the message and repent—namely, the hope of eternal life in the World to Come.

> *For if Joshua had given them rest, God would not have spoken of another day later on.* (HEBREWS 4:8)

The generation of Moses perished in the wilderness, just as the psalm says, "I swore in my wrath, they shall not enter my rest." Joshua led the subsequent generation into the land of Canaan and conquered it. That is to say, he led them into the promised rest (*menuchah*), i.e., the land of Israel. If that is so, why did David declare to his generation that they should beware of hardening their hearts lest they fail to enter God's rest? Were the people in David's time not already living in the land of Israel, that is, in the land of God's rest? The exhorter takes this incongruity as an indication that Psalm 95 must have a different day of rest in view. He deduces that the psalm speaks of the coming Day of the LORD, the kingdom, and the World to Come, which are likened to the Sabbath day.

Incidentally, the Greek name for Joshua is *Ieusous* (i.e., Jesus), which explains the puzzling King James translation of 4:8: "For if Jesus had given them rest, then would he not afterward have spoken of another day." The coincidence in names is not lost on the exhorter. He warns his readers that if they harden their hearts and disobey the good news brought by Yeshua, they will fare no better than the generation of Moses that rejected the good-news message proclaimed by Joshua. If they heed Yeshua's good-news message, they will enter the kingdom and the World to Come just as the subsequent generation in the wilderness followed Joshua into the promised land.

So then, there remains a Sabbath rest for the people of God. (HEBREWS 4:9)

The Sabbath rest that remains for the people of God is the redemption, the kingdom, and the World to Come. The weekly Sabbath offers a foretaste of that future reward and a rehearsal of the goodness that God has stored up for the righteous. This saying does not imply that the weekly Sabbath has been canceled or replaced by a spiritual Sabbath. Instead, the exhorter assumes that his Jewish readers were Sabbath observant Jews and would understand the spiritual significance of their Sabbath observance in a new light—a symbol of their future hope of entering into God's eternal rest.

CHAPTER TEN:
A SABBATH REST REMAINS
(HEBREWS 4:9–13)

> The exhortation of Psalm 95 urges the generation to heed the Messiah, repent, and enter the ultimate Sabbath rest of the kingdom and the World to Come.

I once had a meeting with a pastor of a large evangelical mega-church where I was a teacher in the adult education program. The subject of this particular meeting had to do with some classes that were coming up; I was scheduled to teach about the biblical Sabbath and the festivals. He had recently attended *Jars of Clay*, a First Fruits of Zion conference. The pastor had concerns that I might try to start a Sabbatarian movement in his church. This was several years before I worked with First Fruits of Zion, but I was already guilty by association with Messianic Judaism.

The pastor spoke frankly with me, saying, "I think it's fine if people want to keep the Sabbath as a spiritual discipline, so long as they do not become legalistic about it. They need to understand that we do not have to keep the Sabbath because, as it says in Hebrews 4, Christ is our Sabbath rest now." He was referring to the following passage:

> So then, there remains a Sabbath rest for the people of God, for whoever has entered God's rest has also rested from his works as God did from his. Let us therefore strive to enter that rest. (Hebrews 4:9-11)

According to the pastor's interpretation of Hebrews 4:9, Christ has replaced the Sabbath. From his perspective, people observed a weekly Sabbath day in Old Testament times, but now, in New Testament times, Christ is our Sabbath. That's a good example of how replacement theology works. When it comes to defending replacement theology's abolition of the Sabbath, Hebrews 4 tends to be one of the first places that Bible teachers will turn. They like to use Hebrews 3 and 4 as evidence that a spiritual Sabbath has replaced the literal seventh-day Sabbath rest for the people of God.

I did not bother trying to argue with the pastor. Theological arguments rarely bear good fruit, and I was not in a position to correct a senior pastor's reading of the Bible. However, since this passage is frequently used to defend replacement theology, it will be useful to establish a solid understanding of the text. As demonstrated in the previous chapter, to understand Hebrews 3 and 4, we need to understand Psalm 95. To understand Psalm 95, we need to understand the story of Israel entering the land of Canaan. This chapter builds on the discussion of Hebrews 3:7–4:9, laid out in the previous chapter.

A Taste of the Kingdom

Before the children of Israel entered the land of Canaan, they sent twelve spies to explore the land. The twelve spies went out in midsummer, during the season of the grape harvest. They cut a cluster of grapes so large that they had to carry it on a pole between two men. They brought the giant grapes, some pomegranates, and some figs back to Moses and the children of Israel so they could sample the land.

Ten spies returned with a bad report. They spoke of military fortifications, walled cities, and giant Canaanites. They advised the people to return to Egypt. Two spies, Joshua and Caleb, offered good reports. They said the land was very good. They encouraged the people to trust God, obey him, and enter the land.

Ultimately, the people listened to the ten spies and ignored the advice of Joshua and Caleb. The LORD punished that generation by consigning them to remain in the wilderness for forty years. He did not let them enter the promised land until the entire generation had perished.

The good report of Joshua and Caleb corresponds to the good news that Yeshua and his apostles proclaimed. Just as Joshua and Caleb urged their generation to obey and enter the land, Yeshua and the apostles urged their generation to repent and enter the kingdom.

The story of the spies carrying a cluster of giant grapes back to Moses and the children of Israel foreshadows the days of the apostles. Our Master Yeshua and his twelve disciples brought the first fruits of the kingdom to their generation. Those who saw the miracles of Yeshua and experienced the work of the Spirit through his hands—those fortunate souls tasted the fruit of the age to come.

Although the children of Israel saw the evidence of the goodness of the land of Canaan, they nevertheless refused to listen to the encouraging counsel of Joshua and Caleb. They misinterpreted the enormous fruit as nothing more than evidence of the presence of giants. They hardened their hearts and refused to accept the good report.

Likewise, in the days of the Master, Yeshua's generation rejected his call to repentance. Though they saw his miraculous works, they hardened their hearts and refused to heed him:

> Therefore I was provoked with that generation, and said, "They always go astray in their heart; they have not known my ways." As I swore in my wrath, "They shall not enter my rest." (Hebrews 3:10-11, quoting Psalm 95:10-11)

In the previous chapter, we saw that the words of Psalm 95:11, "they shall not enter my rest," lend themselves to three possible interpretations:

1. They shall not enter my Sabbath rest.
2. They shall not enter my promised land.
3. They shall not enter my kingdom or the World to Come.

Which one of these three possible interpretations does the exhorter have in mind when he quotes the psalm? Does he see the *menuchah* of the LORD as the Sabbath rest, the promised land, or eternal life? The question creates a false trichotomy. We don't have to assume that the exhorter has just one interpretation in mind. In fact, Hebrews 3 and 4 employ all three associations listed above because, in Jewish interpretation, both the weekly Sabbath and the land of Israel correspond to the coming Messianic Era and the World to Come.

The exhorter compares his own generation to the generation of Moses. Both generations stood poised on the edge of attaining the final redemption. The generation of Moses stood at the border of the promised land. The sages teach that if Moses had brought them into Canaan, they would have enjoyed the kingdom immediately. The generation of the Master also stood at the edge of the kingdom. If they had heeded Yeshua's message of the gospel and repented, they would have entered the kingdom of heaven. The Messianic Era hung within their grasp.

Don't Forfeit the Kingdom

Both the generation in the wilderness and the generation of the Master forfeited their opportunity to enter the kingdom. On the other hand, some people from the generation of Moses did enter the promised land. Those who had faith (Joshua and Caleb) received their inheritance. The exhorter compared the disciples of Yeshua in his generation to Joshua and Caleb. Those who have faith (the disciples) will yet enter the kingdom. He warns them not to let go of their confidence. He quotes Psalm 95:7: "Today, if you hear his voice, do not harden your hearts."

Jewish tradition purports that the weekly Sabbath celebrates the coming of the Messiah. The Sabbath offers a weekly foretaste of the coming era of peace and rest—the era when Messiah will rule the earth. By keeping the Sabbath, Jewish people participate in the kingdom of heaven on earth even now. The Sabbath may be likened to a down payment on the age of Messiah yet to come.

Similarly, the land of Israel represents the kingdom. It is the place where the promises of the kingdom will be fulfilled. All the prophecies about the kingdom are about the land of Israel. Israel will be chief over the nations, and Jerusalem will be established as the capital of all people. Even in the World to Come, the Holy Land is not forgotten; the great city that comes down from heaven is called New Jerusalem. So both the land and the Sabbath symbolize the kingdom of heaven and the World to Come.

Today, If You Will Hear

"Today, if you hear his voice, do not harden your hearts," the psalm says. To "hear God's voice" means to obey him. Translating the idiom into easy English, it means, "Today, if you will obey me." The exhorter warns the believers in his generation not to have "an evil, unbelieving heart" like the generation in the wilderness. He says, "For good news came to us just as to them, but the message they heard did not benefit them, because they were not united by faith with those who listened" (Hebrews 4:2). This refers to the good news that Joshua and Caleb brought concerning the land of Israel. The exhorter warns that just as God did not spare the generation of the wilderness, neither would he spare the current generation. He compares entering the land to entering the kingdom. Both require faith and obedience:

> Those who were disobedient ... were not able to enter because of unbelief. (Hebrews 3:18–19)

The epistle goes on to point out that the promised "rest" from which God barred the generation in the wilderness cannot be understood merely as the weekly Sabbath day of rest because God's "works were finished from the foundation of the world" (Hebrews 4:3). Likewise, it cannot refer merely to the promised land, because David wrote Psalm 95 long after Joshua settled the nation in the promised land:

> If Joshua had given them rest, God would not have spoken of another day later on. So then, there remains a Sabbath rest for the people of God. (Hebrews 4:8–9)

The Messianic Kingdom and the World to Come "remain" for those who cling to Yeshua and do not turn away from the living God. Contrary to common interpretation, this does not in any way imply a cessation of the biblical Sabbath or its replacement by a spiritual Sabbath. Instead, the author of Hebrews invokes the Sabbath to symbolize the kingdom and the World to Come, just as the sages did, as explained above.

> *For whoever has entered God's rest has also rested from his works as God did from his.* (HEBREWS 4:10)

The one who observes the Sabbath rests from his labors on the seventh day, just as God rested from his labors after the six days of creation. Likewise, one who obtains the kingdom and a portion in the World to Come will find spiritual restoration and eternal life.

Yeshua declared, "Come to me, all who labor and are heavy laden, and I will give you rest" (Matthew 11:28). One who refuses to enter God's rest continues under the weary labors of this present world.

Be careful not to conflate Hebrews 4:10 with Paul's discussions about faith and works. The exhorter does not have any of those discussions in view. Hebrews 4:10 is not speaking about resting from "works of the Law" or from works of righteousness to rely on grace. Paul's concerns about Gentiles and the Law are not under discussion in Hebrews 4.

Let us therefore strive to enter that rest, so that no one may fall by the same sort of disobedience. (HEBREWS 4:11)

The generation in the wilderness did not perish in its entirety. Caleb and Joshua, the two men who expressed their faith, entered the land of Canaan. The rest of the generation did not. So too, those who believe and repent today will enter the Sabbath rest of the Messianic Era and the World to Come.

The exhorter says that we must "strive to enter that rest." Those who keep a traditional Sabbath are better equipped to understand the picture. When the Sabbath is coming, the traditional Jewish household strives to prepare for its arrival. The members of the household hurry, hustle, scurry, clean, prepare, cook, wash, and work. When the Sabbath finally arrives, the work stops. It is finished. The household members cease from the labor, even if what needs to be done isn't finished. Quiet, calm, and peace enter. Whether your work is done or not, whether you finished everything that needed to be done or not, the Sabbath arrives. The advent of the Sabbath is not contingent on the successful completion of our preparations. We strive to prepare for entering the rest. When Sabbath comes, then we rest.

Does this imply salvation through works? As stated above, the exhorter does not have any such Pauline categories in view, nor is he concerned with any contradiction between faith and works. Even though a person can have complete confidence in God's grace and mercy, he should nevertheless live his life on earth as if entering salvation depended on his efforts. When we finally cross the threshold into the World to Come, we will look back and realize that we accomplished very little, certainly not enough to merit the reward of eternal life. At that point, however, the Sabbath rest will already have begun, and we will already have entered it. Salvation is always by grace.

Nevertheless, disobedience can disqualify us from entering that rest. The exhorter warns his readers that if they imitate the generation of Moses and turn from the Messiah, they will "fall" like the generation "whose bodies fell in the wilderness" (Hebrews 3:17).

For the word of God is living and active, sharper than any two-edged sword. (HEBREWS 4:12)

The exhorter warns his readers not to become lax in their allegiance to Yeshua. They must strive to enter the Sabbath rest that remains for the people of God lest they fall into the same type of unbelieving disobedience that caused the generation of Moses to forfeit the promised land. The "word of God" will judge them not just on the basis of their deeds but also on the basis of "the thoughts and intentions of the heart."

What does the exhorter mean by the term "word of God"? We typically understand this term to refer to the Bible, but that's not the precise meaning here. More broadly, a "word of God" is simply a message from God, and in this case, it should be understood specifically as the good news (gospel) message about Yeshua, repentance in his name, and the coming Day of the LORD. It's the word "spoken to us by his Son, whom he appointed the heir of all things" (Hebrews 1:2). The apostles compared the word of Messiah to a sword. Isaiah describes the mouth of the Messiah as "a sharp sword" (Isaiah 49:2). The book of Revelation develops that imagery further: "From his mouth comes a sharp sword" (Revelation 19:15).

It's fair also to apply the statement more broadly to the Torah, the Prophets, and the Writings (Tanach), which "long ago, at many times and in many ways, God spoke to our fathers by the prophets" (Hebrews 1:1). Paul employs a similar turn of phrase in Ephesians 6:17: "The sword of the Spirit, which is the word of God." The rabbis compared the Torah to a sword on the basis of a Hebrew wordplay. The alternate name for Mount Sinai, on which God gave the Torah to Israel, is Mount Horeb, which sounds like the Hebrew word for "sword." In the context of Hebrews 4, however, the term "Word of God" should be understood as "message from God," specifically the message of the gospel announced by Yeshua.

> *Piercing to the division of soul and of spirit, of*
> *joints and of marrow, and discerning the thoughts*
> *and intentions of the heart.* (HEBREWS 4:12)

One who reneges on his convictions, fails to remain faithful to the message of Yeshua, and abandons his confession of the Messiah will be judged by the one who can see past all pretense and hypocrisy. His gaze slices through all rationalizations and self-justifications to expose the truth. The Word of God divides soul (*nefesh*) and spirit (*ruach*) as easily as a double-edged sword separates "joints and marrow." To derive the truth, the Word of God examines the human psyche, separating between the egoic animal sense of self (*nefesh*) and the ineffable indwelling spiritual being (*ruach*) that preexisted the human body and lives on after death. Human deceits and pretenses do not fool God. Those who shrink back from their convictions about Yeshua under social pressure or for the sake of prestige in the eyes of men will be exposed.

> *And no creature is hidden from his sight, but*
> *all are naked and exposed to the eyes of him to*
> *whom we must give account.* (HEBREWS 4:13)

The exhorter alludes to the story of Adam and Eve hiding from the presence of God in Eden. Though they tried to cover their nakedness and conceal themselves, the LORD sought them out, discovered them, and forced them to "give account." As a consequence of their sin, the LORD exiled them from Eden, barring the way of their return to Paradise with a flaming sword:

> He drove out the man, and at the east of the garden of Eden
> he placed the cherubim and a flaming sword that turned
> every way to guard the way to the tree of life. (Genesis 3:24)

The exhorter warns his readers, by implication, that if they do not hold fast to their confession of Yeshua, their inconstancy will likewise be revealed in the coming apocalyptic day of judgment, and, like Adam and Eve, they will forfeit Paradise. This line of reasoning should be compared with Yeshua's own warning:

Whoever denies me before men, I also will deny before my Father who is in heaven. Do not think that I have come to bring peace to the earth. I have not come to bring peace, but a sword. (Matthew 10:33-34)

What Will You Eat on the Sabbath?

The exhorter warns his readers to repent now to prepare for the kingdom. He warns them not to be like the unbelieving generation in the wilderness that turned away from the good news that Joshua and Caleb brought. Like Hebrews 3 and 4, the following rabbinic parable uses Sabbath symbolism to demonstrate the efficacy of repentance in preparing for the hereafter:

> Consider the case of two wicked men who associated with one another in this world. One of them repented before his death while the other did not repent. It was found that the one stands in the company of the righteous while his fellow stands in the company of the wicked. When the latter saw the former he said, "Woe is me! Is there then favor shown here? I and he, both of us were robbers, both of us were murders together, yet he stands in the company of the righteous and I stand in the company of the wicked!"
>
> The angels said (to the man in Gehenna), "You fool ... you also had the opportunity of repenting and you did not take it." When he heard this, he said to them, "Permit me to go and repent now!" And they answered him and said, "You fool! Do you not know that this world is like the Sabbath and the world from which you have just come is like the eve of the Sabbath? If a man does not prepare his meal on the eve of the Sabbath, what shall he eat on the Sabbath?" (*Ruth Rabbah* 3:3)

A Spiritual Sabbath in Christ

The explanations above reveal that the book of Hebrews uses the Sabbath day and the land of Israel as symbols for the kingdom of heaven and the World to Come. In other words, entering the Sabbath rest and entering the land of Israel are two different metaphors for entering the kingdom and attaining eternal life. However, the metaphors are not intended to supplant the literal observance of the Sabbath or the significance of the literal, physical land of Israel, as my pastor assumed.

I did not bother trying to work through this long explanation of the "Sabbath rest that still remains" with my pastor. The Hebrew terminology and rabbinic parallels were more involved than he would have been prepared to navigate. Nevertheless, it's essential for Messianic Jews and Gentile disciples honoring the Sabbath to have at least a cursory understanding of this passage so we will not be shaken by arguments invoking Hebrews 3 and 4 against the holy day. If nothing else, it is crucial to understand that these chapters do not replace Sabbath observance with a spiritual Sabbath in Christ or some type of realized eschatology.

Instead, the exhorter uses the Sabbath as a metaphor to speak about the future coming kingdom because the Sabbath day was familiar territory for the original readers of the epistle. They were all Jewish disciples of Yeshua, well-accustomed to observing the Sabbath:

> On the Sabbath they rested according to the commandment. (Luke 23:56)

CHAPTER ELEVEN:
THE MESSIANIC PSALM
(HEBREWS 4:14–16)

The apostolic community interpreted
Psalm 110 as a prophecy about the Messiah
seated at the right hand of Glory.

The exhorter introduced his readers to the central argument of his exhortation beginning in Hebrews 4:14: Yeshua, the Son of God, has ascended to become a great high priest in the heavenly Sanctuary. Therefore, we should hold fast to our convictions about him and not allow outside pressures to influence us otherwise.

The hope in the heavenly high priest would have been particularly meaningful to the original readers of the epistle, especially if they were the Greek-speaking cohort of Jewish believers in Judea centered in Jerusalem. In the last decade before the destruction of the Temple, they suffered the martyrdom of their bishop, James, the brother of Yeshua, as well as the execution of several other prominent community members. We have surmised that they might have recently been excommunicated from the assembly and banned from the Temple precinct. The Sadducean high priest Annas the son of Annas inflicted all those injuries.

Today, after two thousand years without the Temple and priesthood, the problem seems less critical, but excommunication and loss of access to the Temple could only have been catastrophic for the first-century believers. It would have put the disciples under enormous pressure to renounce their allegiance to Yeshua. Unless they did, they could not find their way back into fellowship with the congregation of Israel and good standing with the high priesthood. In view of that tension, the question of access to the priesthood became an acute crisis for the community. The Epistle to the Hebrews attempts to offer a solution for the divorce between the Levitical priesthood and the disciples of Yeshua.

Encounter with the Sadducees

The disciples of Yeshua never had a good relationship with the Sadducean high priesthood. Yeshua warned them, "Remember the word that I said to you: 'A servant is not greater than his master.' If they persecuted me, they will also persecute you" (John 15:20). The Sadducees, who denied the resurrection of the dead and the existence of the divine soul, hated the Master and persecuted him, and they treated his disciples in the same manner. The high priest, Caiaphas, orchestrated the crucifixion of Yeshua and set the course for the high priesthood's ongoing campaign against the disciples.

Mark 11 relates the story of an encounter between Yeshua and Caiaphas:

> They came again to Jerusalem. And as he was walking in the temple, the chief priests and the scribes and the elders came to him, and they said to him, "By what authority are you doing these things, or who gave you this authority to do them?" (Mark 11:27-28)

In those days, it was not unusual for the prominent sages of the Sanhedrin to teach in the Temple courts during the festivals, but who was this upstart from Galilee? How did he merit that privilege? Yeshua dodged their question, but he could not completely escape the religious authorities, the chief priests, the teachers of the Torah, and the elders. For most of Mark 12, they harassed him with questions devised to expose some theological or political flaw by which they might disqualify him as Messiah.

He had satisfactorily answered all of their questions, but they still had not found a way to entrap or disqualify him. Then Yeshua turned the tables and asked them, "How can the scribes say that the [Messiah] is the son of David?" (Mark 12:35). This seemed like an absurd question. Obviously, the Messiah must be the son of David, otherwise he cannot be the Messiah. The Messiah must sit on his father David's throne and restore the Davidic monarchy in order to fulfill the prophecies. The teachers of the Torah knew it; the people in the Temple listening to the discussion knew it; Yeshua knew it; everyone knew it. But Yeshua turned their attention to the cryptic words of Psalm 110:

> David himself, in the Holy Spirit, declared, "The Lord said to my Lord, 'Sit at my right hand, until I put your enemies under your feet.'" (Mark 12:36)

The sages believed that David uttered all his psalms under the divine inspiration of the Holy Spirit. They understood Psalm 110 as a prophecy about the Messiah. So did the apostles. The apostles quoted Psalm 110 more than any other passage of the Hebrew Scriptures—fifteen times in the New Testament directly, with several more allusions to the psalm along the way. Of those fifteen citations, nine appear in the Epistle to the Hebrews. We already encountered one of them in Hebrews 1:13: "To which of the angels did God ever say: 'Sit at my right hand until I make your enemies a footstool for your feet?'" The apostles used Psalm 110 to validate their convictions about the ascended Messiah seated at the right hand of the Father.

Whose Son?

In his confrontation with the chief priests in the Temple, the Master quoted Psalm 110 to explain his premise that the Messiah cannot be *merely* the son of David. As Rabbi Yeshua read the psalm, he noticed that King David referred to the coming Messiah (whom God would seat at his right hand) as "my master." How could a father (David) call his own son (Messiah Son of David) "my master"? Yeshua used this reversal of protocol to argue that the Messiah must be more than merely a Davidic heir.

His argument is unintelligible when reading the psalm in English (or Greek) because the translations do not distinguish between the circumlocution for the name of God and the common word "Lord." To get the proper sense of the passage and to eliminate the ambiguity created by translation, the paraphrase below will read *HaShem* where the original Hebrew text has the name of God and the word "master" where the Hebrew has the word for "lord" (*adon*):

> A Psalm of David. [David says,] HaShem says to my master: "Sit at my right hand, until I make your enemies your footstool." HaShem sends forth from Zion your mighty scepter. Rule in the midst of your enemies! Your people will offer themselves freely on the day of your power, in holy garments; from the womb of the morning, the dew of your youth will be yours. HaShem has sworn and will not change his mind, "You are a priest forever after the order of Melchizedek." The master is at HaShem's right hand; he will shatter kings on the day of his wrath. He will execute judgment among the nations, filling them with corpses; he will shatter chiefs over the wide earth. He will drink from the brook by the way; therefore he will lift up his head. (Psalm 110, paraphrase)

An early rabbinic teaching presents a similar interpretation of the psalm. In this version, the "my master" character is the Messiah, but this time, Father Abraham is the one calling the Messiah "my master." When Abraham sees that his son, the Messiah, is seated at HaShem's right hand, whereas he himself sits at HaShem's left hand, the reversal of proper protocol offends him. How is it that his son is honored above him?

> In the time to come, the Holy One, blessed be He, will seat the Messiah King on his right and Abraham on his left. Then the face of Abraham will become jealous, and he will say, "My grandson sits on the right and I sit on the left?" Then the Holy One, blessed be He, will appease him, saying, "Your grandson sits on your right and I am on your right." (*Yalkut Shimoni* on Psalm 110)

The midrash demonstrates that Yeshua was not the only one to interpret Psalm 110 in such a fashion. He did not deny the Davidic ancestry of the Messiah. Neither did the midrash in *Yalkut Shimoni* mean to propose that the Messiah might not be a literal son of Abraham. Rather, just as the midrash does, Yeshua pointed out the incongruous reversal in father-son protocol. The Messiah must be more than merely a Davidic heir descended from the Davidic line, or his father David would not refer to him as "my master." The Messiah takes a seat at the right hand of God. If he were merely David's son, he would be seated at the right hand of David. If he is seated at the right hand of

HaShem, whose son is the Messiah? This is the puzzle Yeshua posed in reply to the question the chief priests put to him, "By whose authority do you do these things?"

The questioners who tried to stump Yeshua found themselves stumped. Whose son, then, is the Messiah? Two prophecies about the Davidic dynasty provided further clues:

> When your days are fulfilled and you lie down with your fathers, I will raise up your offspring after you, who shall come from your body, and I will establish his kingdom. He shall build a house for my name, and I will establish the throne of his kingdom forever. *I will be to him a father, and he shall be to me a son.* (2 Samuel 7:12-14, emphasis mine)

> I will tell of the decree: The LORD said to me, "*You are my Son; today I have begotten you.* Ask of me, and I will make the nations your heritage, and the ends of the earth your possession." (Psalm 2:7-8, emphasis mine)

The Messiah Priest

The Sadducean high priesthood in the Temple demanded of Yeshua, "By what authority are you doing these things, and who gave you authority to do this?" Just as Messiah is greater than David (because David calls the Messiah master and the Messiah is seated at the right hand of God), so too, he is greater than the Aaronic priesthood.

The Messiah derives his authority directly from God, and his priesthood is likened to that of Melchizedek. Psalm 110, the same psalm that seats Messiah at the right hand of God, also declares that the Messiah is "a priest in the order of Melchizedek."

Perhaps this seems like an evasive way to answer the question about authority, but it was direct enough to get Yeshua killed. When he stood trial before the Sadducees a day or so later, Caiaphas brought up this incident. Frustrated because of his inability to find even a single pretense for executing Yeshua, Caiaphas recalled the encounter in the Temple courts during which Yeshua had taught on Psalm 110 and seemed to apply the message of the psalm to himself. Hadn't he claimed that he was Messiah and, as in the psalm, taken a seat at the right hand of God? Hadn't he been claiming to be more than merely the son of David? Hadn't he claimed to be the son of God? Caiaphas asked, "Are you the Messiah, the Son of the Blessed One?"

Yeshua replied, "I am, and you will see the Son of Man *seated at the right hand* of Power" (Mark 14:62, emphasis mine). When Caiaphas heard those words, he tore his garments and issued a blasphemy verdict.

> *Since then we have a great high priest who has passed through the heavens, [Yeshua], the Son of God, let us hold fast our confession.* (HEBREWS 4:14)

The exchange over the meaning of Psalm 110 and the identity of the Messiah as the Son of God was well-known and familiar material to the Jewish disciples. The entire incident, which resulted in Yeshua's crucifixion and his ensuing resurrection, was foundational to the Yeshua narrative and formative in the community's theology of Messiah.

The exhorter turns to that same well-known and often-exegeted Psalm 110 to draw out a new insight. Not only does Psalm 110 identify the Messiah as the Son of God seated at the right hand of HaShem, but it also refers to him as a high priest in the order of Melchizedek—a priestly status that transcends the earthly office occupied by Caiaphas and the elitist Sadducean priesthood. The exhorter rhetorically asks, "Would it be wise to renounce your allegiance to Yeshua and lose your connection to his heavenly priesthood for the sake of obtaining the approval of an earthly priesthood?" Instead, he argues, they should hold fast to their confession.

> *For we do not have a high priest who is unable to sympathize with our weaknesses, but one who in every respect has been tempted as we are, yet without sin.* (HEBREWS 4:15)

Earlier in the epistle, the exhorter unabashedly advanced his theology about the divine identity of the Messiah. He said that the Messiah is "the heir of all things, through whom also [God] created the world. He is the radiance of the glory of God and the exact imprint of his nature, and he upholds the universe by the word of his power"

(Hebrews 1:2-3). But it is not the divine transcendent character of the supernal man or the heavenly personification of divine wisdom to which the exhorter draws the reader's attention in 4:15. Instead, he points to Yeshua's humanity.

It is not his inner divine nature that grants Yeshua the ability to sympathize with human beings and connect with imperfect and sinful people. Like the sons of Aaron who mediate between God and Israel, Yeshua was (and is) a real human being, a man who felt hunger, thirst, pain, and every frailty. He knew anger, frustration, joy, humor, love, and passion, just as we do. He knew what it was to experience heartbreak, loss, fear, and loneliness. He laughed as we laugh and was tempted "in every respect" as we are. He sympathizes with human weakness because he is human and has experienced weakness himself. Unlike the sons of Aaron who serve in the earthly priesthood, Yeshua transcended human weakness. Though tempted in every respect, he remained without sin and entered sinless into the immortal state. In a show of ultimate empathy for his fellow human beings, he diagnosed the human disorder in the words, "Father, forgive them, for they know not what they do" (Luke 23:34).

Let us then with confidence draw near to the throne of grace, that we may receive mercy and find grace to help in time of need. (HEBREWS 4:16)

The ark of the covenant that once stood within the holy of holies of the Temple symbolized God's throne. The LORD sat enthroned between the cherubim upon "the mercy seat." The exhorter referred to "the mercy seat" as "the throne of grace." Those seeking God's help and mercy prayed toward the Temple, offered sacrifices, and sent a priest on their behalf to stand before the throne of grace and atone for them in the presence of God. We have surmised that, in the last decade before the destruction of the Temple, the Sadducean-dominated priesthood excluded the disciples of Yeshua from participating in those rites. They excluded them from the benefit of priestly atonement, denying them access to the house of God and the throne of grace.

The exhorter encourages his readers to draw close to God through the agency of the sympathetic priesthood of Melchizedek, occupied by the risen and exalted Messiah, Yeshua of Nazareth. Although they could no longer rely on the mediation of an earthly priesthood, they could confidently rely on the heavenly priesthood of Yeshua. Through the agency of his priesthood, they would "receive mercy and find grace in time of need."

CHAPTER TWELVE:
THE SOURCE OF ETERNAL SALVATION
(HEBREWS 5:1–10)

The messianic prophecies of Psalms 2 and 110 indicate that Messiah has been named Son and high priest in the order of Melchizedek.

A few years before the outbreak of the Jewish Revolt, the Sadducean high priesthood that controlled the Temple in Jerusalem took aggressive measures against the disciples of Yeshua. They put to death James the Righteous and several of the Master's most prominent followers. At the same time, they attempted to have Solomon's Portico, the eastern colonnade of the Temple Mount where the disciples were accustomed to assemble daily, dismantled for reconstruction. We speculated that around the same time, the high priesthood banned the disciples of Yeshua from the Temple, cutting them off from access to the holy house of God, from the sacrifices, the worship, and the priesthood. This situation precipitated a crisis for the believers. Imagine how the community of Yeshua's disciples must have felt when the Day of Atonement arrived. They knew the high priest, who went into the holy of holies as the representative and intercessor of all Israel, had deliberately excluded them from the atonement ceremony. All Israel looked to the high priest as the hope of the people. He entered where no else could tread, and he reconciled the nation to God. The Torah says, "On this day shall atonement be made for you to cleanse you. You shall be clean before the LORD from all your sins" (Leviticus 16:30).

We have speculated that the exhorter addressed his word of exhortation to the Greek-speaking Jewish community to address that crisis. He called for perseverance: "Hold fast to the confession of Yeshua." He also offered a theological consolation by presenting the priesthood of Messiah, as if to say, "Although you are separated from the Levitical priesthood and can no longer benefit from their atoning work, you have a high priest in the heavenly Temple, Yeshua of Nazareth, who serves as a priest in the order of Melchizedek."

For every high priest chosen from among men is appointed to act on behalf of men in relation to God, to offer gifts and sacrifices for sins. (HEBREWS 5:1)

The exhorter begins a discussion about the role of a high priest with a view toward Aaron, the brother of Moses and the progenitor of the high priesthood. The original readers of the epistle were already aware that the Torah's Hebrew term for the office of the high priest is *kohen haMashiach*, i.e., "the anointed priest" or, to put it even more pointedly, "the messiah priest."

In the Levitical hierarchy, a priest from the order of Aaron receives the privilege of an anointing that sets him in an office above the rest of the priesthood. He is to serve the nation as a mediator. He represents human beings before God. He offers various gifts and offerings and sacrifices on behalf of the layman. He has permission to enter the holy places of the Sanctuary, where the layman cannot go. He brings the blood of sin offerings into the innermost place and thereby effects atonement on behalf of others.

He can deal gently with the ignorant and wayward, since he himself is beset with weakness. (HEBREWS 5:2)

The high priest is not chosen for his position on the basis of moral superiority over the laymen he represents. He is not more righteous or spiritually exalted than the average Israelite. Instead, he is of the same character as the common non-priest, sharing the same weaknesses and frailties. That commonality gives him empathy for his fellow man. Jewish tradition painted the character of Aaron, the first high priest, in similar strokes:

> Hillel said: "Be a disciple of Aaron, loving peace, pursuing peace, loving and bringing all creatures near to the Torah." (m.*Avot* 1:11)

The sages spoke fondly of Aaron's love for every Jew. His compassion for his fellow sprang from his close identification with the layman. Aaron could empathize with people and deal gently with the ignorant and wayward because he himself was beset with weakness. Psalm 133 idealizes Aaron's love for his fellow Israelites:

> Behold, how good and pleasant it is when brothers dwell in unity! It is like the precious oil on the head, running down on the beard, on the beard of Aaron, running down on the collar of his robes! (Psalm 133:1–2)

Because of this he is obligated to offer sacrifice for his own sins just as he does for those of the people. (HEBREWS 5:3)

According to the exhorter, a worthy priest must empathize with the laymen he represents. If so, Aaron's transgression in the incident of the golden calf prepared him to be an effective high priest. Aaron could empathize with people because he understood what it was to be guilty of a grievous sin.

On the other hand, the advantage of being a sinner like other sinners also limits the efficaciousness of the priesthood. The priest from the order of Aaron had his own sins and transgressions separating him from God. An imperfect human being could hardly be expected to perfect others. A sinful human being could not properly represent the holy and righteous God; neither could he atone for others when he had his own sins that needed atonement.

> *And no one takes this honor for himself, but only when called by God, just as Aaron was.* (HEBREWS 5:4)

How does the exhorter derive the idea that Yeshua is a priest at all, much less a high priest? He observes that no one can achieve the honor or appoint himself to the position. It must be conferred upon a person by God, as was the case with Moses' brother, Aaron.

A Roman Catholic male can become a priest by attending seminary and taking the sacred vows of priesthood. The Jewish priesthood does not work that way. The Torah's laws limit participation in the Levitical priesthood to Aaron's family, and the descendants of Aaron are responsible for filling the office. The Torah warns, "If any outsider comes near, he shall be put to death" (Numbers 1:51). By "outsider," the Torah means anyone outside of Aaron's family.

In the days of Hillel and Shammai, a certain Gentile idolater heard about the extravagant vestments worn by the high priest of Israel. He decided he wanted to become a Jew so that he could become the high priest and don such splendor:

> Then the Gentile said to himself, "I will go and become a proselyte so that I may be appointed a high priest." He went before Shammai and said to him, "Make me a proselyte on the condition that you appoint me to the position of high priest." Shammai repulsed him with the builder's cubit which was in his hand. He then went before Hillel, who made him a proselyte. Hillel said to the man, "Can anyone be made a king if he does not know the rules of the kingdom? Go and study the rules of the kingdom!" He went and studied the Torah. When he came to the passage that says, "If any outsider comes near, he shall be put to death," he asked Hillel, "To whom does this verse apply?" "Even to David, king of Israel," Hillel answered. Thereupon the proselyte reasoned within himself from the light to the heavy: "The people of Israel are called sons of God, and, in His great love for them, God referred to them as 'Israel is my son, my firstborn.' If it is written of them, 'If any outsider comes near, he shall be put to death,' how much more so a mere proselyte, who comes with his staff and wallet!" He returned to Shammai and said

to him, "Was I ever eligible to be a high priest? Does the Torah not say, 'If any outsider comes near, he shall be put to death'?" He went before Hillel and said to him, "O gentle Hillel; blessings rest on your head for bringing me under the wings of the Divine Presence!" (b.*Shabbat* 31a)

The above story illustrates that even if David, the king of Israel, wanted to become a priest, he could not. Only the sons of Aaron qualify for the priesthood. If so, how can Yeshua, a descendant of the tribe of Judah and a son of the house of David, be called a priest? King Uzziah, also a son of David, once tried to take on a priestly function. He attempted to offer incense in the Holy Temple along with the priests. The LORD was merciful to him and only struck him with leprosy. He lived the rest of his days outside the city as a leper. Not even a son of David, the king of Israel, can occupy the priestly office. Only the sons of Aaron qualify for the Levitical priesthood.

Given the exclusive nature of the Aaronic priesthood, how could Yeshua be considered a priest? The exhorter has to answer this objection before advancing his premise. He points to another priest of God Most High who was *not* a son of Aaron: Melchizedek, the king of Salem. The exhorter now begins his argument to prove that Yeshua qualifies for this other priesthood outside of the Aaronic priesthood.

> *So also [Messiah] did not exalt himself to be made a high priest, but was appointed by him who said to him, "You are my Son, today I have begotten you"; as he says also in another place, "You are a priest forever, after the order of Melchizedek."* (HEBREWS 5:5-6)

The exhorter quotes two seemingly unrelated passages to prove that the Messiah is a priest belonging to the order of Melchizedek:

> I will tell of the decree: The LORD said to me, "You are my Son; today I have begotten you." (Psalms 2:7)

> The LORD has sworn and will not change his mind, "You are a priest forever after the order of Melchizedek." (Psalms 110:4)

In the previous chapter, we explored the messianic content of Psalm 110, a psalm that Judaism closely associates with the Messiah. Traditional Jewish interpretation also identifies Psalm 2 as a prophetic psalm about the Messiah. It explicitly mentions the LORD's Messiah (*mashiach*): "The kings of the earth set themselves, and the rulers take counsel together, against the LORD and against his Anointed [*Mashiach*]" (Psalm 2:2). On a literal level, Psalm 2 could apply to any Davidic king because all the sons of David were called anointed ones. The psalm might originally have been composed for David, Solomon, Hezekiah, or Josiah. By the time of the apostles, however, the Jewish people interpreted Psalm 2 with specific reference to the last Davidic King: King Messiah. According to its traditional interpretation, Psalm 2 pertains to the coming Messiah and the apocalyptic end-times war called the battle of Gog and Magog.

Psalm 2 has several similarities to Psalm 110. Judaism applies both psalms to the Messiah. Both psalms talk about God establishing his anointed king in Zion. Both refer to the rod of iron or the mighty scepter that King Messiah will use to rule over the nations. Both make predictions about God subjugating all nations under King Messiah. And (most significant for interpreting Hebrews 5) both contain a direct address to the Messiah. That is to say, both psalms present God speaking directly to the Messiah in the form of an oracular declaration.

The writer of the book of Hebrews uses the messianic interpretation of Psalm 2 as the foundation of his argument from Psalm 110. He juxtaposes the two texts to argue that if we accept that the Messiah is called the Son of God on the authority of Psalm 2, then we must also accept that he is also a priest in the order of Melchizedek on the authority of Psalm 110.

God speaks directly to the Messiah in both psalms, addressing him with the second-person pronoun "you." (In Hebrew, it's the pronoun *attah*.)

- Psalm 2: "You are My Son. *Beni attah*."
- Psalm 110: "You are a priest. *Attah kohen*."

In this apostolic midrash on the text, the exhorter uses the Hebrew pronoun *attah* as if it is a title for the Messiah: You.

"*Attah*, You are My Son. *Attah*, You are a Priest."

The same God who said, "You are my son, today I have begotten you," also said, "You are a priest forever after the order of Melchizedek." Thus, the Messiah did not seek his priesthood himself or take it upon himself. Just as in the case of Aaron the brother of Moses, God appointed him to it.

> *In the days of his flesh, [Yeshua] offered up prayers and supplications, with loud cries and tears, to him who was able to save him from death.* (HEBREWS 5:7)

At what point did the Messiah become "a priest forever after the order of Melchizedek?" The writer of Hebrews explains that it happened through the transformation of his resurrection. He refers to the period of time before Yeshua's resurrection as "the days of his flesh," i.e., his normal human body. In that mortal state, Yeshua prayed passionately for salvation from death. The exhorter specifically references the Master's prayers in Gethsemane on the night before he suffered: "Father, if you are willing, take this cup from me, but not my will but your will." Facing the cross, he prayed through to the resurrection.

Hebrews 5:7 preserves an apostolic memory of the prayer life of our Master. Yeshua prayed with loud cries and tears. He prayed passionately, intensely, in great agony; he threw himself into prayer. He prayed in private because, for him, prayer was sometimes a loud thing. The Master prayed intimately, crying out, "Abba, Father!" He prayed with absolute intention and focus. Yeshua offered a model of prayer that his disciples should aspire to emulate.

> *And he was heard because of his reverence.* (HEBREWS 5:7)

The exhorter connects Yeshua's resurrection and victory over death to his fervent prayers in Gethsemane. God heard the prayers of Yeshua "because of his reverence," which would be better translated as "because of his fear [of the LORD]." The fear of the LORD is the conviction that God punishes sin and rewards righteousness. One possessing the fear of the LORD conducts himself in righteousness and shuns sin. Yeshua's prayers and pleas were heard because he feared God and lived a life of sinless righteousness.

A passage from the Talmud offers a similar story about the resurrection of the Messiah. In the story, there are two messiahs at work bringing the redemption. The Messiah son of Joseph suffers and dies on Israel's behalf as predicted in Isaiah 53. The Messiah son of David brings the kingdom and establishes the Messianic Era. In the story, the Messiah son of Joseph dies fighting for Israel in the battle against Gog and Magog. The Messiah son of David prays for him, asking God to resurrect the slain suffering servant. The Talmud interprets Psalm 21:5(4) as the prayer offered by the Messiah son of David when he asks God to rescue the Messiah son of Joseph from death: "He asked life of you; you gave it to him, length of days forever and ever." In the talmudic story, God capitulates, answers the Messiah's prayer, and resurrects Messiah son of Joseph from the dead (b.*Sukkot* 52a).

Although he was a son, he learned obedience through what he suffered. (HEBREWS 5:8)

The exhorter points back to Psalm 2, where God declared to the Messiah, "You are my son." The Messiah did not attain his resurrection and heavenly priesthood merely as a right of privilege based on his sonship. He needed to first pass through sufferings and trials to prove his allegiance and obedience to his Heavenly Father. Yeshua submitted himself to suffering; he took up his cross and carried it. He chose to lose his life so that he might find it, and through his suffering, he was made "perfect." He obtained the resurrection and the heavenly declaration, "You are a priest forever after the order of Melchizedek."

And being made perfect, he became the source of eternal salvation to all who obey him, being designated by God a high priest after the order of Melchizedek. (HEBREWS 5:9-10)

Yeshua was made perfect through suffering. Wasn't he already perfect? The exhorter refers not to an improvement in his moral character, but to the transition of his body from the mortal state to the immortal state. "Being made perfect" means passing from death to life and from corruptible mortal flesh to incorruptible, immortal flesh. As we have observed in previous chapters, the "perfect" is the resurrection.

Only after entering the undying state of his resurrected body did he qualify to fulfill the words of Psalm 110: "You are a priest forever." In that capacity, he became the source of eternal salvation to all who obey him. Those who heed his teaching and cleave to him will also obtain a share in the resurrection and the World to Come.

Because he lives forever as the eternal Son and the eternal priest, he has become the source of eternal salvation to all who heed him. The exhorter uses the term "eternal salvation" to distinguish the resurrection of the dead from the broader concept of national redemption. He has in view more than Israel's redemption from exile and oppression of the nations. The term "eternal salvation" refers to obtaining a share in the World to Come through the power of resurrection.

CHAPTER THIRTEEN:
ELEMENTARY PRINCIPLES
(HEBREWS 5:11–6:3)

> Six elementary principles summarize the gospel message and constitute the milk of the Word of God.

Do you consider yourself a spiritual person? A seasoned believer and educated disciple? Before you answer, consider the apostles' prerequisite for such an appellation: mastery of the basic principles of the oracles of God. If we still need someone to teach us the elementary doctrine of the Messiah, we are unskilled in the Word of righteousness and still need milk. We are not yet ready for solid food.

About this we have much to say, and it is hard to explain, since you have become dull of hearing. (HEBREWS 5:11)

After presenting his readers with the material we discussed in the previous chapter, the exhorter wants to continue the discourse with additional insights along the same lines. He says, "About this we have much to say." He probably wants to further discuss the work of Messiah, his eternal priesthood, and the mysterious, mystical, priestly order of Melchizedek. However, he feels frustrated because his readership seems unprepared for those more profound spiritual lessons. The exhorter wants to go deep, but his readers are still swimming in the shallows. He complains, "It is hard to explain, since you have become dull of hearing." They do not yet have the basics down.

> *For though by this time you ought to be teachers, you need someone to teach you again the basic principles of the oracles of God. You need milk, not solid food. For everyone who lives on milk is unskilled in the word of righteousness, since he is a child.* (HEBREWS 5:12-13)

The exhorter wants to feed his readers meat and potatoes, but he fears they might be unable to digest them. He considers his readers, as yet, spiritually immature, like children still at the breast, far past the age when they should have been weaned. It's as if he is saying, *I want to give you some heavy teaching, but you still need to learn the ABCs.*

The Apostle Paul expresses a similar frustration in his epistle to the Corinthians:

> But I, brothers, could not address you as spiritual people, but as people of the flesh, as infants in [Messiah]. I fed you with milk, not solid food, for you were not ready for it. And even now you are not yet ready. (1 Corinthians 3:1-2)

Apparently, the original Jewish readers of the Epistle to the Hebrews needed to spiritually grow before they could begin to grasp the deep things of Messiah. But hold on a minute. Is that really true? Were the readers of this epistle really "infants in Messiah"?

The Epistle to the Hebrews contains some of the most difficult material in the New Testament. Our study so far has revealed multiple layers of complexity and sophisticated biblical allusions employing rabbinic methods of argumentation. The exhorter assumed that his readership understood what he was writing, but he wrote at a level of biblical literacy that far surpasses our own today. He expected his readers to recognize and understand subtle allusions to numerous Old Testament passages. He bandied about quotations from the Torah, the Psalms, and the Prophets in a sort of apostolic shorthand to invoke whole concepts and inter-textual relationships. He employed rabbinic modes of exegesis and argumentation that required his readers to be well-studied and adept in those forms of discourse. So what did he mean by saying to his readers, "You still need milk"?

> *But solid food is for the mature, for those*
> *who have their powers of discernment*
> *trained by constant practice to distinguish*
> *good from evil.* (HEBREWS 5:14)

The exhorter hesitates to plow ahead into his mystical discourse on Yeshua, Melchizedek, the Temple, and the priesthood because he ordinarily reserves such esoteric subjects for "the mature." He defines the mature as those who have, through godly living and a consistent life of discipleship, learned to distinguish "good from evil" and to apply that distinction in their moral choices. The Jewish believers in the Hebrews community still need milk: "the basic principles of the oracles of God."

If that kind of teaching was what the exhorter called "milk," then what are we drinking today? What passes for deep, spiritual education in our generation isn't even real milk; instead, it's the spiritual equivalent of nutritionally deficient baby formula. It's a collection of doctrines and dogmas that presuppose no fundamental biblical literacy and never go deeper than a few centimeters.

> *Therefore let us leave the elementary doctrine of*
> *[Messiah] and go on to maturity.* (HEBREWS 6:1)

The exhorter refers to the milk—the baby stuff—as the elementary teachings about Messiah. Another way of saying that would be "the basics of Christian faith." Even better and less anachronistically, we could call it "the basic teachings of the Messiah."

As I read Hebrews 6:1-2, I count six of these basic teachings. The exhorter calls these basic doctrines "foundations." You might call this passage an apostolic catechism:

> Therefore let us leave the elementary doctrine of [Messiah] and go on to maturity, not laying again a foundation of [1] repentance from dead works and of [2] faith toward God, and of [3] instruction about washings, [4] the laying on of hands, [5] the resurrection of the dead, and [6] eternal judgment. (Hebrews 6:1-2)

1. Repentance from dead works
2. Faith toward God
3. Instruction about washings
4. The laying on of hands
5. The resurrection of the dead
6. Eternal judgment

Do we have a good handle on all these? Have we got this stuff down? We do not. Almost two thousand years later, we have even less of a clue about these six foundations than the readers of the epistle possessed. Let's briefly overview the six fundamental teachings of the Messiah.

Not laying again a foundation of repentance from dead works. (HEBREWS 6:1)

The book of Hebrews lists repentance from dead works as the first basic teaching of Messiah. Protestants often read this one backward to mean repentance from attempts to earn salvation through righteous living, specifically from observing the rituals and ceremonies of Judaism. According to that opinion, the term "dead works" refers to godliness and obedience to the commandments in the Old Testament. It's not uncommon for a teacher or a pastor to conflate Hebrews 6:1 with Pauline discussions about works of the Law and then explain the first foundational, elementary doctrine of Christ—the most fundamental teaching of Christianity—as repentance from keeping the Law. That is, repentance from works because "no one is saved by works but only by grace through faith."

On the contrary, "dead works" is another name for sin, not for obedience to the Law. Paul said, "The wages of sin is death" (Romans 6:23). The Torah itself says, "I have set before you life and death, blessings and curses. Now choose life, so that you and your children may live" (Deuteronomy 30:19 NIV). Sin is the agent of death. Through sin, death came into the world.

To suppose one should repent from obeying God's commandments is to misunderstand the meaning of the word "repentance"—to stop sinning, turn around, and start walking according to God's instructions. Moses taught repentance. The prophets taught repentance. In the days of our Master, even the Pharisees taught repentance.

The exhorter calls repentance an elementary teaching of Messiah because the gospel message started with a call to repentance. One might even say that repentance is the essential gospel message. The gospel story begins with John the Immerser, preparing "the Way," calling out, "Repent, for the kingdom of heaven is at hand" (Matthew 3:2). That message runs consistently through the teachings of Yeshua and the whole New Testament.

Most Evangelical Christians today believe that the gospel message is "Believe in Jesus, and you will go to heaven when you die." Is that what Yeshua preached? Is that what Yeshua told his twelve disciples to proclaim as he sent them out to preach? Did he say, "As you go, proclaim this message: 'Believe in Jesus, and you will go to heaven when you die'"? That's not what the Bible says. Maybe that's what his teaching means, but the real message of the gospel that he entrusted to his disciples and taught them to proclaim was the same message that he had been teaching from the beginning and that John had been teaching as well:

> John the Baptist came preaching in the wilderness of Judea, "Repent, for the kingdom of heaven is at hand." (Matthew 3:1-2)

> From that time [Yeshua] began to preach, saying, "Repent, for the kingdom of heaven is at hand." (Matthew 4:17)

> These twelve [Yeshua] sent out, instructing them, "... Proclaim as you go, saying, 'The kingdom of heaven is at hand.'" (Matthew 10:5-7)

Repentance is an elementary teaching of Messiah. To teach that repentance from dead works means to turn away from God's commandments is not only bizarre and backward; it's satanic. Even the milk isn't being taught anymore. We're feeding our babies poison from the bottle.

And of faith toward God. (HEBREWS 6:1)

The foundational teaching of faith toward God seems obvious enough: You have to believe in God to be a disciple, right? *Faith* in God is not the same as *belief* in God. James, the brother of Yeshua, said that even the demons believe, but assuredly the demons are neither Christians nor disciples of Yeshua. What is faith toward God?

In the long interval between my first and second series of sermons through Hebrews, I read Matthew W. Bates' remarkable monograph, *Salvation by Allegiance Alone: Rethinking Faith, Works, and the Gospel of Jesus the King*. Bates argues persuasively that the Greek word (*pistis*) that we translate as "faith" and "belief" is sometimes better translated as allegiance and loyalty to a monarch. This single insight reconciles a host of difficulties and seeming discrepancies in New Testament exegesis and helps clarify Hebrews 6:1.

As a fundamental teaching of the Messiah, faith toward God should be understood as the type of radical allegiance to God taught and modeled by Yeshua. Yeshua taught his disciples to rely on God completely and always prioritize his kingdom ahead of their own needs and concerns. The loyalty toward God taught by Yeshua exceeded the religious piety of the day. He said, "Unless your righteousness exceeds that of the scribes and Pharisees, you will never enter the kingdom of heaven" (Matthew 5:20). He taught his disciples to go beyond the letter of the law, exercising a constant fear of the LORD. He taught a radical level of allegiance to God.

While it is also true that "faith is the assurance of things hoped for, the conviction of things not seen" (Hebrews 11:1), it's precisely because the coming kingdom remains unseen and only hoped for that we must retain our allegiance to the King. Even though we do not yet see the kingdom revealed in this world, we maintain our confident loyalty to God, trusting that he is in control, punishes sin, and rewards righteousness, whether in this life or the next. This type of allegiance entails the fear of the LORD because "without faith it is impossible to please him, for whoever would draw near to God must believe that he exists and that he rewards those who seek him" (Hebrews 11:6). It should disturb us to hear teaching about God that tries to undermine this principle. Grace-preachers love to quote Isaiah 64:6: "All our righteous deeds are like a polluted garment," and then they declare, "All our sins are forgiven by grace." As a result, many Christians believe in a God who does not reward righteousness or punish sin.

It is true that we find forgiveness and reconciliation by the grace of God that he bestowed upon his Son. By the merit of our Master's suffering, we have the forgiveness of sins and hope for eternal life. But that does not in any way imply that God is no longer in the business of punishing sin and rewarding righteousness. True faith toward God trusts that he both punishes and rewards, whether in this life or the next, and that he is in control—and more than that, he is good. This is the God revealed to us through the Scriptures and the teaching of Yeshua.

And of instruction about washings. (HEBREWS 6:2)

The book of Hebrews lists "instruction about washings" as the third basic teaching of the Messiah. Other English translations render it "instruction about baptisms." Both translations are correct because we derive the word "baptism" from the Greek word (*baptismo*) for "washing" and "immersing." Notice that the exhorter did not say "instruction about baptism"; he said "instruction about baptisms."

In the days of the apostles, Jewish people knew about baptism. Jewish people in Jerusalem underwent a ceremonial immersion every time they entered the Temple. They immersed themselves to remove Levitical defilement. The Bible required people visiting the Temple in Jerusalem to go through a ceremonial immersion before they could enter God's house. Some people, such as the priests, immersed themselves every day.

Even today, some pious Jews immerse themselves prior to Sabbaths and festivals. To prepare for marriage, both the bride and the groom go through a baptism for ritual purity on the night before their wedding day. Married women undergo a similar immersion at least once a month. Those who wash the dead in preparation for burial go through an immersion before and after the ceremonial washing of the corpse. They wash the corpse to prepare it for the resurrection. Judaism employs many different types of "baptisms," which is why the English Standard Version avoids the word "baptism" with all its Christian, sacramental associations and translates the Greek *baptismo* as "washings."

In keeping with the Jewish mode of immersion for ceremonial purification, John the Baptist introduced a baptism of repentance. He told people to confess their sins, repent, and immerse themselves. The apostles called on people to confess their sins and immerse themselves in the name of Yeshua.

When Christianity broke free from her Jewish moorings, the ceremony of baptism evolved into a sacramental rite, and the church abandoned the Jewish form of the immersion ritual. The Anabaptists of the Reformation Era attempted to restore the original Jewish version of the ritual, but even among Protestants, to this very day, Christians debate the significance, symbolism, and procedure of baptism. Division over baptism continues to segment Christianity and polarize churches.

In light of the baptism debates, one might assume that instruction about washings refers to instructions on how to administer the ceremony of baptism. On the contrary, that cannot be the concern the exhorter had in mind. Why would the apostles need to give Jewish believers instructions about how to conduct immersions? It makes no sense to think that this elementary principle of faith in Messiah could have been about how to use a mikvah (ceremonial bathing pool). Every first-century Jew knew how to conduct an immersion.

Instead, "the instruction" refers to the basic teachings of Yeshua that the apostles presented to people before immersing them. One might think of the instruction as an early catechism. In the nineteenth century, scholars rediscovered a first-century "instruction about baptisms" that the apostolic community had created for new Gentile disciples to study prior to undergoing baptism. The Greek document is titled *The Instruction of the Master to the Gentiles through the Twelve Apostles*. It is called the *Didache* for short, which means *The Instruction*. It consists primarily of an introductory course of apostolic instruction in the teachings and sayings of our Master that a person learned before undergoing an immersion in his name. We could think of it as a *Discipleship 101* course. The apostles considered that type of instruction before baptism to be elementary—the milk fed to new believers.

The laying on of hands. (HEBREWS 6:2)

The institution of the laying on of hands also comes from the Torah and Jewish practice. In the Temple, a man laid his hands on the head of the animal he was about to sacrifice so that it would be accepted and identified on his behalf. In the Torah, Moses laid hands on Joshua to install him as the new leader. Several other examples occur in the Tanach.

The Jewish sages and teachers of Torah in the Apostolic Era also used the ritual to confer discipleship. A sage laid hands on his disciples to ordain them as teachers. The rabbis speak of a chain of tradition and ordination by which one generation passes the torch of Torah to the next. This is what the laying on of hands means in this context. It refers to the Jewish custom of initiating a new disciple.

For example, when Timothy first became a disciple of Yeshua, the council of elders in his congregation laid hands on him and prophesied over him. Paul said to Timothy, "Do not neglect the gift you have, which was given you by prophecy when the council of elders laid their hands on you" (1 Timothy 4:14). In the same epistle, Paul warned Timothy, "Do not be hasty in the laying on of hands, nor take part in the sins of others; keep yourself pure" (1 Timothy 5:22). In other words, "Don't be too quick to accept new disciples into the fold," or, perhaps, "Don't be too quick to appoint elders in the congregations." Both interpretations work.

The laying on of hands signifies entrance into discipleship. It symbolizes an investment of Yeshua's identity through the power and authority of his name. The apostles based it on a common Jewish practice that appears in the Torah. It is milk; it is basic stuff.

The resurrection of the dead. (HEBREWS 6:2)

The foundational teaching of the resurrection of the dead simply means that there will be a resurrection. The doctrine has implications for us before death and ramifications for us after death. The teaching of the resurrection of the dead includes discussion about who gets resurrected, on what criteria, when, and so forth. Jews in the first century hotly debated these questions. The Sadducees (who did not believe in a resurrection) hated the followers of Yeshua primarily because they championed faith in the resurrection.

Traditional Jews consider a firm faith in the resurrection of the dead as fundamental to Judaism. Maimonides called it one of the thirteen basic principles of Jewish faith. How much more should we consider it a basic principle of faith for disciples of the risen Messiah?

I am astonished at how many Bible teachers neglect and ignore the doctrine of the resurrection from the dead. Many find it difficult to reconcile it with the popular view of an eternal home in heaven. Despite our allegiance to the resurrected Yeshua, we ignore the doctrine of resurrection, shove it under the table, and hide it in the closet. You will hear plenty of sermons about going to heaven and spending eternity in glory, but no one talks much about the hope of the resurrection. Few seem to understand it. The hope of the resurrection embarrasses modern sensibilities as if the modern thinker is too sophisticated for such a primitive Hebrew superstition. We talk happily about going to heaven to be with Grandma, but the whole expectation of a literal, physical resurrection of the dead seems pretty murky. Nevertheless, every Easter, Christians gather to revel in the resurrection of Yeshua.

Why all this confused ambiguity about something so central to our faith? The doctrine of the resurrection of the dead should be a basic assumption. It is milk—something so fundamental to us that we should not need to explain it to people who call themselves Christians.

And eternal judgment. (HEBREWS 6:2)

The final foundational doctrine in the series of six is the eternal judgment. It refers to the Pharisaic belief that we will all receive our comeuppance (or our reward) not just in this world but primarily in the next world—the next life. The doctrine of eternal judgment teaches that God will distribute divine punishment and reward to human beings in the afterlife. This world is merely a vestibule for the World to Come, and a person should prepare himself (or herself) in the vestibule so that he (or she) will be ready to enter the banquet hall. Repent now; work hard to enter into the eternal rest of Messiah because there is an eye that sees and an ear that hears, and all your deeds are written in a book.

The doctrine of the eternal judgment entails the belief that every human being will stand before the judgment, that the heavenly court will open books of judgment, and that ultimately, everyone will receive a verdict and find his name recorded either in the Book of Life or the Book of Death: the eternal verdict. Belief in the final, eternal judgment permeates all the teachings of Yeshua and the New Testament. It was one of the foundational beliefs of Apostolic-era believers. It is milk; it is basic stuff. This is just the initiation.

The Basic Gospel

On closer examination, the six doctrines sketch out the hope of the gospel and the proper response to it. They call us to follow Yeshua, seek entrance to the kingdom of heaven, and receive the final reward.

1. REPENTANCE: Repent in the name of Yeshua; turn away from sin; turn back to God's instruction for your life, because the kingdom is at hand.

2. FAITH TOWARD GOD: You are saved by grace through faith, and you must express your faith toward God by living it in radical allegiance to him.

3. INSTRUCTION ABOUT WASHINGS: Therefore, as a symbol of your repentance and entrance into the kingdom, be immersed in the name of Yeshua. Before you do that, however, you should learn some of the teachings of Yeshua so that you understand the life to which you are committing yourself.

4. LAYING ON OF HANDS: After your immersion, enter into the ranks of discipleship under the authority of the elders of your local congregation as they invest you with the laying on of hands.

5. RESURRECTION OF THE DEAD: As a disciple, you will live out the life of the resurrected Messiah now as you eagerly anticipate your own resurrection.

6. ETERNAL JUDGMENT: After the resurrection, you will face eternal judgment. If you are in Messiah, having complied with steps one through five, you will find forgiveness, pardon, and entrance into eternal life.

These six doctrines outline the response that a person should have toward the gospel message. This is the milk of the Word—the basic stuff. I am astonished when I look at this simple gospel protocol as recorded in the New Testament and realize how very few points of contact still exist between these six basic principles of Messiah and the conventional message that passes for the gospel in today's churches. The exhorter said, "Therefore let us leave the elementary doctrine of

[Messiah] and go on to maturity. ... And this we will do if God permits" (Hebrews 6:1-3).

For more specific teaching on each of the six principles, see my book *Elementary Principles: Six Foundational Principles of Ancient Jewish Christianity*, which further develops each subject.

CHAPTER FOURTEEN:
THINGS THAT BELONG TO SALVATION
(HEBREWS 6:4–12)

It's possible to fall away from Yeshua and forfeit the World to Come, but the one who endures to the end will be saved.

Hebrews 6:4–8 is a difficult passage that has inspired millennia of debate. It appears to teach that if a disciple drifts away from the faith and denies the Master, there is no coming back. It seems there is no possibility of repentance for lapsed Christians or those who deny Yeshua. Is it really possible for a Christian to fall from grace and forfeit salvation? Is there a point at which God slams the gates of heaven closed to repentance?

As Far as the East Is from the West

The early church wanted to know the answers to those questions, too. The interpretation of Hebrews 6:4–8 became so controversial that much of the church resisted canonizing the book of Hebrews. Second-century conservative Roman Christians like Tertullian rigidly understood the passage to mean that after baptism, one is never presented with another opportunity to repent for sins. When a new Christian received baptism, the water washed away sins committed previously as a non-Christian, but any sins committed after baptism were not forgiven and could jeopardize salvation. This was the majority interpretation in second- and third-century Christianity.

After the Decian persecution (249–250 CE), the rigorist conservatives used the passage to argue that persecuted Christians who had recanted their faith under persecution could not be forgiven and readmitted to the church. Eventually, a softer interpretation won the day; while baptism itself was still understood as a one-time-only, unrepeatable event in the life of a believer, repentance and forgiveness were still possible throughout one's life. This remains the majority opinion.

Meanwhile, in the Eastern Christian world, no similar controversy over Hebrews 6:4–8 arose. The Eastern church's lack of concern over the passage illustrates one of many differences between Eastern and Western forms of Christianity. Westerners treat Scripture in strictly analytical and logical ways, like a math problem, where every component of the equation has constant values, and the only trick is to figure out the correct answers to the variables. The Eastern mind can hold concepts more loosely and allows for unresolved tension to remain between texts—even tolerating contradictions.

I'm a Westerner who has worked hard to learn to read the text from an Eastern mindset. When I read Hebrews 6:4–8, it no longer troubles me. As I see it, the exhorter warned the Jewish disciples not to fall away from their allegiance to Yeshua lest they find themselves forever unable to return to him. I would not recommend attempting to derive a universal doctrine of eternal security (or eternal insecurity, as the case may be) from a passage like this. That's not the point. It's a dire warning, spoken like a prophet of old; the exhorter was not trying to teach a systematic theology of soteriology.

What Have We Got to Lose?

I try to avoid the eternal security debate. Salvation, reward and punishment, the final redemption, Paradise, Gehenna, the resurrection, the kingdom, the World to Come, and the final judgment are presented in a much more nuanced way in the Scriptures than the dogmas generated by systematic theologies would have us believe. None of these ideas fits easily into the free-grace box of once-saved-always-saved. I don't think the apostles even had a box like that.

On the other hand, there is a story about my father that I love to tell because it illustrates his gentle wisdom and keen insight into the human heart. One of the men in his church in Granite Falls, Minnesota, came to him and said, "Pastor, I've been studying it out with a few of the men, and we've come to the conclusion that there is no eternal security and that a person can lose his salvation." My father replied in his gentle manner and ironic sense of humor, "Well, if you can lose your salvation, you certainly will, and probably already have." That is to say, if maintaining one's favor with God depends on the personal righteousness of the individual, we are all in a lot of trouble.

My father had a solid grasp of God's grace. He did not need anyone to tell him what was in a man's heart; he knew because he understood that sin dwells in the hearts of everyone, even the redeemed. The Apostle Paul was acutely aware of the waywardness in his own heart when he wrote, "Sin dwells within me ... nothing good dwells in me ... the law of sin dwells in my members, I serve the Torah of God with my mind, but with my flesh I serve the law of sin." Any person who does not recognize that fundamental truth about the human condition must be blind to his own deficiencies. If we say we are without sin, we deceive ourselves, and the truth is not in us. Salvation was by God's grace before we were saved; it is by grace after we are saved; it will be by God's grace when we fall asleep in death, and it will be by God's grace when he awakens us from the slumber of death.

Consequently, we are not going to delve into the theological controversy over whether salvation can be lost. Instead, we will learn what we stand to lose outside of Messiah, and why we should never consider abandoning our allegiance to Yeshua.

Attributes of the Disciple

What does it mean to be a disciple of Yeshua? Hebrews 6:3-5 lists five attributes that characterize the spiritual experience of the believer:

> Therefore let us leave the elementary doctrine of [Messiah] and go on to maturity ... And this we will do if God permits. For it is impossible, in the case of those who have once been enlightened, who have tasted the heavenly gift, and have shared in the Holy Spirit, and have tasted the goodness of the word of God and the powers of the age to come. (Hebrews 6:1, 3-5)

According to this passage, the disciple of Yeshua is one who has:

- Been enlightened.
- Tasted the heavenly gift.
- Shared in the Holy Spirit.
- Tasted the goodness of the word of God.
- Tasted the powers of the age to come.

All five attributes relate to the hope of the Messianic Era and the World to Come, and all five merit further consideration. The exhorter warned that one who has experienced these five gifts through faith in Yeshua is thereafter held accountable. As the Master himself put it, "Everyone to whom much was given, of him much will be required, and from him to whom they entrusted much, they will demand the more" (Luke 12:48).

For it is impossible, in the case of those who have once been enlightened. (HEBREWS 6:4)

Enlightenment refers to knowledge of God and relationship with God. Yeshua told his disciples, "To you it has been given to know the secrets of the kingdom of heaven, but to them it has not been given" (Matthew 13:11). In the Messianic Era, the knowledge of God will be universal:

> No longer shall each one teach his neighbor and each his brother, saying, "Know the LORD," for they shall all know me, from the least of them to the greatest. (Jeremiah 31:34)

> The earth shall be full of the knowledge of the LORD as the waters cover the sea. (Isaiah 11:9)

The full culmination of this revelation is reserved for the Messianic Era: "Now I know in part, then I shall know fully, even as I have been fully known" (1 Corinthians 13:12).

The enlightened person has been brought out of the dark ignorance of idolatry, materialism, and agnosticism and received a little bit of the light of revelation. Through the teaching of Yeshua and the evidence of his resurrection, the enlightened person has obtained knowledge of God and the certainty of the spiritual truths unveiled by the prophets. God is involved with the world. He is going to redeem Israel and all humanity. We are spiritual beings and must live by faith. We are certain of a final judgment, reward and punishment in the afterlife, the kingdom, and the World to Come. The enlightened person has received a small portion of the knowledge and experience of God that will become universal in the Messianic Age and the World to Come.

Who have tasted the heavenly gift. (HEBREWS 6:4)

The enlightened person has "tasted the heavenly gift," meaning that this person has experienced, in some small measure, the blessings that will be universal in the kingdom and the World to Come. For example, a state of world peace will govern the Messianic Era. The disciple of Yeshua should possess a portion of that future peace in the form of the inner peace that passes understanding that our Master bequeathed to his disciples. The same principle applies to all the promises of the kingdom. Yeshua taught us to ask God for "the bread of tomorrow," i.e., to ask for the substance of the future kingdom in our lives today.

This is not the same as realized eschatology, which posits that the Christian receives all the promises of the eschatological kingdom now in this world through Christ. Instead, we are speaking of a foretaste of the future glory yet to come. One who "tastes" something does not consume the whole amount. A taste of the heavenly gift implies that there is much more of the same to be enjoyed in the future. A pious Jewish tradition recommends tasting the Sabbath soup on Friday afternoon before the Sabbath begins. It's a way to bring some flavor of the Sabbath's holiness into the world before the holy day arrives. This custom illustrates the idea that the Sabbath offers us a foretaste of the kingdom and the World to Come.

Repentance from sin and allegiance to Yeshua grant us a foretaste of the banquet table of the Messianic Era. Personal salvation can be considered a foretaste of the final redemption, and that includes a down payment on the good promises of the Messianic Era.

And have shared in the Holy Spirit. (HEBREWS 6:4)

The enlightened person has "shared in the Holy Spirit." The endowment of the Holy Spirit offers a specific example of the general idea of having "tasted of the heavenly gift." In the Messianic Era, the Holy Spirit will be poured out on all humanity (Joel 3:1-2[2:28-29]). Everyone will receive direct spiritual communication from God in the form of prophecy, visions, and dreams. The greatest prophets in this current era are of lower prophetic caliber than the least among the prophets of the Messianic Era. But the disciples of Yeshua are eligible to receive a foretaste of that future universal revelation of God's Spirit. The apostles explained the outpouring of the Spirit in Acts 2 as the beginning of the fulfillment of that future universal outpouring. Disciples of Yeshua receive a share of the Spirit that rested on the Master, much as Elisha received a double portion of the Spirit of God that rested on Elijah. We experience God's Spirit in the manifestation of the fruit of the Spirit, in spiritual gifts, and spiritual insights of wisdom, discernment, and knowledge. Yet this experience of the Spirit is merely a down payment on and a small share of the future endowment. This is why Paul refers to the Holy Spirit as a "pledge" of the fullness yet to come.

And have tasted the goodness of the word of God. (HEBREWS 6:5)

The enlightened person has "tasted the goodness of the word of God." The term "word of God" should be understood as God's message. In this context, "word of God" implies the message spoken by Yeshua: "In these last days he has spoken to us by his Son, whom he appointed the heir of all things" (Hebrews 1:2). By experiencing a foretaste of the future Messianic Era and the World to Come, the disciple of Yeshua experiences some of the nearness of the kingdom Yeshua proclaimed. Moreover, the disciple takes a foretaste of promises spoken "long ago to the fathers in the prophets in many portions and in many ways" (Hebrews 1:3). For example, spiritual cleansing, the circumcision of the heart, the forgiveness of sins, the knowledge of God, spiritual direction, the indwelling of the Holy Spirit, the fraternity of brothers, physical healing, provision and sustenance, and fertility and abundance are all prophetic promises about the coming kingdom. The disciple of Yeshua lays hold of those future promises as much as possible to bring them to bear upon his life in this current age.

And the powers of the age to come. (HEBREWS 6:5)

The enlightened person tastes "the powers of the age to come." The exhorter consistently conflates the future kingdom (Messianic Era) and the new heavens and the new earth (World to Come). Both eras are implied by his use of the term "age to come" in 6:5. The disciple has received a taste of the powers of the age to come in the form of supernatural miracles, not the least of which is the resurrection of Yeshua. In Jewish liturgy, the "power" of God is demonstrated by the resurrection of the dead:

> You are *powerful* forever, my Master. You resurrect the dead, fully able to save … Who is like you, capable of *powerful* deeds, and who can compare with you? You are a king who causes death and resurrects, and you make salvation sprout forth! (*Shemoneh Esrei* 2)

Even if a believer has not personally seen a miracle with his own eyes, he has seen many through the corporate witness of the disciples. The enlightened person knows the miracles one does see in this world—those inexplicable acts of the power of God that seem to disrupt the natural order—are only momentary incidents in which the future Messianic Era has intruded on this current age. They are merely a small foretaste, a sampling, of God's power that will manifest fully in the kingdom and the World to Come.

And then have fallen away, to restore them again to repentance, since they are crucifying once again the Son of God to their own harm and holding him up to contempt. (HEBREWS 6:6)

The exhorter warns that one who has received all the above foretastes of the future and subsequently apostatizes could be compared to one who crucifies the Master all over again. Why? Because the apostate denies the evidence of Yeshua's resurrection and its implications—leaving his body dead. This person cannot be restored to the fellowship so long as he remains in that state of "crucifying once again the Son of God ... holding him up to contempt." No effort should be expended "to restore them again to repentance" because their apostasy is intentional and belligerent. Because much was given to them, much is required of them. They have fallen into the category of those who deny Yeshua before men; therefore, he denies them before his Father in heaven (Matthew 10:33).

The possibility remains that the apostate himself might repent and seek restoration. God may yet reopen the blind man's eyes a second time or turn the heart back. Hebrews 6:6 does not address the case of an apostate who has repented from apostasy to return to faith.

What Kind of Dirt Am I?

The exhorter creates a brief parable that compares the disciples of Yeshua to different types of soil. The parable is a variation of Yeshua's parable of the sower, which compares four kinds of disciples. The one on whom the seed fell beside the path is the one who hears the message about the kingdom but does not understand it. The evil one snatches away what was sown in his heart. The one on whom the seed fell on the rocky ground is the one who receives the message of the kingdom with joy and immediately sprouts, but he remains only temporarily. When the sun rises, he is scorched because he has no root in himself. His allegiance to Yeshua withers away. The one on whom the seed fell among the thorns is the one who receives the word and understands it, but the worries of the world and the deceitfulness of wealth choke it and make it unfruitful. According to Yeshua's parable, three out of four disciples fail to thrive. It's reminiscent of the old sower's poem: One for the blackbird, one for the crow, one for the cutworm, and one to grow.

> *For land that has drunk the rain that often falls on it, and produces a crop useful to those for whose sake it is cultivated, receives a blessing from God.* (HEBREWS 6:7)

The disciple who remains faithful to Yeshua is like soil that produces a crop. The rain that falls on the soil symbolizes the heavenly gift, the endowment of the Spirit, the goodness of the kingdom message, and the experience of the miracles of the coming age. The sower who cultivates the soil represents Yeshua and his disciples, who proclaim the good news of the kingdom. The crop ripe for harvest refers to a faithful course of discipleship lived out. The blessing from God symbolizes reward in the age to come.

> *But if it bears thorns and thistles, it is worthless and near to being cursed, and its end is to be burned.* (HEBREWS 6:8)

The apostate is compared to land that drinks rain from heaven but bears no crop except thorns and thistles. In the end, since the land cannot be cultivated to produce a harvest, it will be burned off.

Every disciple should beware of becoming the unfruitful land. You don't want to be the bad dirt, drinking in the rain but producing only thistles and thorns.

In a similar analogy, Yeshua said,

> I am the vine; you are the branches. Whoever abides in me and I in him, he it is that bears much fruit, for apart from me you can do nothing. If anyone does not abide in me he is thrown away like a branch and withers; and the branches are gathered, thrown into the fire, and burned. (John 15:5–6)

In another similar analogy (Matthew 13:24–26, 37–42), Yeshua contrasted different types of disciples as wheat and tares. The tares are weeds that look just like the wheat until the harvest. At the end of the age, the wheat is gathered into barns, but the weeds are bound in bundles and burned in the fire. You don't want to be a weed, and you don't want to be the bad soil.

Does a Weed Know It's a Weed?

I had a friend who grew up in a large Evangelical church. He went to all the youth group events. He told me that despite the Christian atmosphere and all sorts of church events, special speakers, conferences, and retreats, every youth group member was sexually active, and several members were addicted to narcotics. He claimed he felt far less peer pressure from non-Christian kids, who at least respected him as a Christian, than he felt from the Christian kids in his youth group. They were bad soil and weeds. They looked like wheat on the outside, but their deeds were those of weeds.

Does the weed know that it's a weed? I'm pretty sure all those youth group kids were confident of their eternal security because they had followed the prescribed formula of receiving Jesus: "Lord Jesus, come into my heart." It doesn't sound to me as if any of them had cast their allegiance with him or surrendered their lives to him. Weeds usually don't even know that they are weeds. (If you are worried that you might be a weed, it's a pretty good indication that you aren't. Real weeds rarely ever think of themselves as weeds.)

Don't be a weed planted among the wheat. Don't be a branch that does not abide in the vine. Don't be like the ground that drinks in the rain from heaven but produces only thorns and thistles. Don't be like Iscariot, who turned away from the Master.

> *Though we speak in this way, yet in your case, beloved, we feel sure of better things—things that belong to salvation.* (HEBREWS 6:9)

The exhorter speaks in the first-person plural, "we speak in this way," to indicate that his words represent the consensus of the authorities and teachers with him at the time of the composition of the epistle. After issuing such a stern warning about apostasy, he assures his readers of his confidence in their faithful allegiance to Yeshua. They exhibit the godly characteristics of sincere disciples, as described above. They will ultimately bear good fruit and enter the reward of the kingdom and the World to Come. The "things that belong to salvation" are indications of sincere faith and spiritual transformation, namely the "work and the love" demonstrated in the name of Messiah mentioned in

6:10. In this context, "salvation" refers to the full gamut of the future national redemption, resurrection of the dead, and a share in the World to Come. The exhorter sees clear indications that the community is sincere in their faith and allegiance to Yeshua and will participate in that future salvation when the Son of Man comes.

For God is not unjust so as to overlook your work and the love that you have shown for his name in serving the saints, as you still do. (HEBREWS 6:10)

The disciples to whom the epistle is addressed practice selfless service for "the saints," that is, for other disciples of Yeshua. Their expression of love for other believers and the acts of service that they perform for one another indicate that they are neither weeds nor bad soil. Love for others is always the hallmark evidence of sincere allegiance to Yeshua:

> By this all people will know that you are my disciples, if you have love for one another. (John 13:35)

The exhorter assures the disciples that God will reward them for the good works they have done in the name of the Master. Indeed, if God does not do so, he would be unjust. They will receive their reward in the redemption, the kingdom, and the World to Come.

And we desire each one of you to show the same earnestness to have the full assurance of hope until the end. (HEBREWS 6:11)

The exhorter speaks his stern warnings regarding the consequences of apostasy out of a desire to firm up the faith and commitment of each community member. The intention is not to cause the disciples to doubt their future salvation but rather to compel them to lay hold of that hope more firmly. The exhorter wants them to cling tightly to their confession about Yeshua as Messiah and risen King and to exercise their faith in him devoutly so their confidence in the future salvation would not waver. If they do so, they will retain their hope "until the end," that is, until the end of the age. Enduring to "the end" is a common theme in apostolic teaching because Yeshua said, "The one who endures to the end will be saved" (Matthew 24:13).

So that you may not be sluggish, but imitators of those who through faith and patience inherit the promises. (HEBREWS 6:12)

The disciples are in danger of losing their initial zeal for the Messiah. As time goes on and pressure to renounce their allegiance to Yeshua rises, they are apt to lose their enthusiasm and might easily slip into an agnostic type of apathy. The exhorter urges them to imitate instead the tenacity of earlier generations, who "through faith and patience" obtained the prize of eternal life in the World to Come. He returns to that thought in Hebrews 11, where he offers the reader examples of "people of old" who, by faith, "received their commendation" and became heirs "of the righteousness that comes by faith" (Hebrews 11:2, 7). In the current context, the exhorter specifically has in mind Abraham who "having patiently waited, obtained the promise" (Hebrews 6:15). So may it be said of us all.

CHAPTER FIFTEEN:
TWO UNCHANGEABLE THINGS
(HEBREWS 6:13–18)

The disciple of Yeshua has confidence because God must keep the oath he made to Abraham and the oath he made to the Messiah.

King Solomon said, "Hope deferred makes the heart sick, but a desire fulfilled is a tree of life" (Proverbs 13:12). In the last decade before the destruction of the Temple, the Jewish disciples of Yeshua had already had their fill of "hope deferred." During the early days of the Yeshua community, the disciples in Jerusalem gathered daily in Solomon's Colonnade in anticipation of the imminent return of the Son of Man. They waited for "that day his feet shall stand on the Mount of Olives that lies before Jerusalem on the east" (Zechariah 14:4), and they wanted to be among the first to welcome him with shouts of "Hosanna! Blessed is he who comes in the name of the LORD!" They waited and watched as Yeshua had instructed them: "Blessed is that servant whom his master will find so doing when he comes" (Matthew 24:46). But he did not come. Each passing day brought fresh disappointment, deferring hope for another day.

Under threat of persecution, mounting pressure from religious authorities, and perhaps excision from participation in the Temple and its Levitical rites, the community began to buckle. Some members abandoned assembling with other disciples. Others openly renounced their allegiance to Yeshua.

The exhorter warns his readers against apostasy. Dire consequences await those who abandon their hope in the Messiah, for "it is impossible ... to restore them again to repentance" (Hebrews 6:4-6). The exhorter urges his readers to persevere in their faith that they might be counted among "those who through faith and patience inherit the promises" (Hebrews 6:12). He exhorts the disciples to imitate Abraham who, "having patiently waited, obtained the promise" (Hebrews 6:15). If they will do so, he promises, they will find their desire fulfilled in the end—"a tree of life to those who lay hold of her; those who hold her fast are called blessed" (Proverbs 3:18).

The Promise to Abraham

Abraham experienced "hope deferred." By the time Abraham set out for Canaan, he was no longer a young man. The LORD promised to bless him with land, fame, progeny, nationhood, and universal influence. All nations were to be blessed in him. To receive the promises, however, he needed first to leave Mesopotamia and travel to Canaan. Abraham did so. He was already seventy-five years old (Genesis 12:4). God appeared to him again after he arrived in Canaan and promised to give the land to his children, but Abraham had no children. Despite the difficulty, Abraham clung tenaciously to the promise. Years passed. His barren wife, Sarah, remained childless. Abraham refused to relinquish his faith in God's promises. Ultimately, twenty-five years elapsed between Abraham's arrival in Canaan and the birth of the promised son, Isaac: "Abraham was a hundred years old when his son Isaac was born to him" (Genesis 21:5).

At the time the exhorter composed his word of exhortation, the community of disciples to whom he addressed his epistle had already been waiting for the return of Yeshua of Nazareth longer than Abraham had waited for Isaac. For nearly forty years, they waited for the Master to return, bring the final redemption, restore the kingdom, defeat the enemies of Israel, gather in the exiles, and raise the dead for a share in the World to Come. The patient faith of Abraham while he waited for the fulfillment of God's promise provided the community of Yeshua's disciples with a worthy model to emulate:

> He did not weaken in faith when he considered his own body, which was as good as dead (since he was about a hundred years old), or when he considered the barrenness of Sarah's womb. No distrust made him waver concerning the promise of God, but he grew strong in his faith as he gave glory to God, fully convinced that God was able to do what he had promised. (Romans 4:19-21)

The exhorter likewise wanted his readers to exercise such Abrahamic confidence in the coming of Yeshua. He urged them to demonstrate "the full assurance of hope until the end" (Hebrews 6:11).

Paul and Abraham

The exhorter's appeal to the endurance of Abraham sounds similar to Pauline material. Paul frequently directs his readers to consider the faith of Abraham. Paul referred to Abraham as the father of the faith, and he referred to disciples of Yeshua as those who "walk in the footsteps of the faith that our father Abraham had" (Romans 4:12). Paul focused his discussions about the faith of Abraham on one specific story from the life of the patriarch.

In Genesis 15, Abraham complained that he had no children to inherit his possessions or carry on his legacy after him. God brought him out of the tent and showed him the star-filled nighttime sky, saying, "Look toward the heaven, and number the stars, if you are able to number them ... so shall your offspring be." Abraham believed the promise, and God rewarded his faith by crediting him with righteousness:

> Then he said to him, "So shall your offspring be." And he believed the LORD, and he counted it to him as righteousness. (Genesis 15:5-6)

> In hope he believed against hope, that he should become the father of many nations, as he had been told, "So shall your offspring be." (Romans 4:18)

Paul uses that story to illustrate the relationship between faith in Yeshua and righteousness in God's eyes. Because Abraham believed the promise and remained steadfast in his conviction, the LORD regarded Abraham as righteous. Abraham's faith did not waver. "Fully convinced that God was able to do what he had promised. That is why his faith was 'counted to him as righteousness'" (Romans 4:21-22). Yeshua is the promised "offspring" of Abraham. According to Paul's interpretation of the story, the disciple who demonstrates Abrahamic faith by believing the good news about Yeshua and confessing allegiance to the Messiah King receives the forgiveness of sins in his name, thereby obtaining vindication (righteousness) in the eyes of heaven (Romans 4; Galatians 3).

However, whenever Paul cites this story, he always does so intending to prove the efficaciousness of Abraham's faith prior to his circumcision. He does not quote Genesis 15:5-6 as an appeal to the patient endurance of Abraham's faith but rather to offer a proof text supporting his conviction that circumcision cannot be considered a qualification for receiving justification in God's eyes. Since the LORD "counted it to him as righteousness" some twenty-four years before Abraham cut off his foreskin, circumcision cannot be considered a criterion for being numbered among the righteous. Paul's epistles show interest in Abraham's faith only for the sake of Paul's argument for the inclusion of Gentile disciples in the kingdom.

We have already suggested that the exhorter was either a colleague of Paul or a member of his school of influence. If so, it's no surprise to find the exhorter exegeting the same Abraham story along similar lines. However, he does not use the text to argue for the inclusion of Gentiles as Paul did. Instead, the exhorter takes the discussion about Abraham's faith in a different direction. The discussion in Hebrews has more in common with the interpretation offered by James, the brother of the Master, in that the exhorter points readers toward the test of Abraham's faith in the story of the binding of Isaac (Genesis 22).

The Binding of Isaac

"After these things God tested Abraham" (Genesis 22:1). According to James, Abraham did not prove his faith or receive the commendation of righteousness until he passed the test by offering up his son Isaac. Only then was the scripture "fulfilled that says, 'Abraham believed God, and it was counted to him as righteousness'" (James 2:23). *Because* Abraham passed the test by relinquishing his son for the altar, God reiterated the promise to bless him and multiply his offspring "as the stars of heaven." In other words, Abraham was justified (declared righteous) based on deeds, not just a confession of faith:

> Was not Abraham our father justified by works when he offered up his son Isaac on the altar? You see that faith was active along with his works, and faith was completed by his works. (James 2:21-22)

For when God made a promise to Abraham, since he had no one greater by whom to swear, he swore by himself, saying, "Surely I will bless you and multiply you." And thus Abraham, having patiently waited, obtained the promise. (HEBREWS 6:13-15)

The exhorter's interpretation of the story has more in common with James' teaching than with Paul's. The exhorter uses the test in Genesis 22 as evidence of Abraham's faith—the type of faith he wants his readers to emulate. His readership faced a difficult test of faith. Like Abraham, they waited for the fulfillment of a divine promise. Although their hope for the arrival of the Son of Man had been deferred, the exhorter did not want them to despair. The disciples needed to imitate Abraham, who "having patiently waited, obtained the promise" of offspring like the stars of the sky.

Offspring "like the stars of the sky" is the same promise from Genesis 15 that Abraham believed (and it was credited to him as righteousness), but the exhorter draws the promise instead from Genesis 22. He quotes Genesis 22:17: "Surely I will bless you and multiply you." It's a shorthand reference for the full passage in which the LORD reiterates the promise after Abraham passes the test of the binding of Isaac:

> By myself I have sworn, declares the LORD, because you have done this and have not withheld your son, your only son, I will surely bless you, and I *will surely multiply your offspring as the stars of heaven* and as the sand that is on the seashore. And your offspring shall possess the gate of his enemies, and in your offspring shall all the nations of the earth be blessed, because you have obeyed my voice. (Genesis 22:16-18, emphasis mine)

> *For people swear by something greater than themselves, and in all their disputes an oath is final for confirmation.* (HEBREWS 6:16)

After the binding of Isaac, the LORD reiterated his promises to Abraham, and he sealed the promises by adding an oath. An oath was more than just an emphatic way of speaking. In the biblical era, people swore oaths in the name of a deity to legally bind themselves to their promises or to validate their words. For example, "May the LORD do so to me and more if I don't do such and such" (e.g., Ruth 1:17; 1 Kings 2:23). Oath-taking was serious business. The Torah forbids taking oaths in the names of other gods; we are to swear only in the name of the LORD: "By his name you shall swear" (Deuteronomy 6:13); "You shall not swear by my name falsely" (Leviticus 19:12). Anyone swearing falsely in a deity's name invited divine retribution. The writer of the book of Hebrews refers to the practice of taking oaths in the name of a deity when he says, "For people swear by something greater than themselves."

In the days of the apostles, Torah courts of law sometimes asked litigants to take an oath in God's name to validate their claims. In the absence of witnesses or evidence, the court could accept an oath as sufficient grounds to accept a litigant's testimony and to settle a case. Modern legal systems still employ that ancient practice by requiring witnesses to swear upon a holy book. The Talmud gives numerous examples of court cases settled when one party or the other was willing to take an oath to establish the truth of his words. The exhorter also refers to the common courtroom practice of using oaths to settle a legal dispute: "And in all their disputes an oath is final for confirmation" (Hebrews 6:16).

But what if God wanted to take an oath? In whose name would he swear? "Since he had no one greater by whom to swear, he swore by himself," swearing in his own name, "By myself I have sworn, declares the LORD" (Genesis 22:16).

> *So when God desired to show more convincingly to the heirs of the promise the unchangeable character of his purpose, he guaranteed it with an oath.* (HEBREWS 6:17)

The exhorter explains that the LORD took this second oath "to show more convincingly to the heirs of the promise" God made to Abraham his reliability and unswerving commitment to deliver on the promise. In this way, the exhorter juxtaposes the oath that God swore to Abraham with the oath that he swore concerning the Messiah:

> *By myself I have sworn,* declares the LORD ... I will surely bless you, and I will surely multiply your offspring as the stars of heaven (Genesis 22:16-17, emphasis mine).

> *The LORD has sworn* and will not change his mind, "You are a priest forever after the order of Melchizedek." (Psalm 110:4, emphasis mine)

> *So that by two unchangeable things, in which it is impossible for God to lie, we who have fled for refuge might have strong encouragement to hold fast to the hope set before us.* (HEBREWS 6:18)

The exhorter explains that God's sworn oath provides sufficient grounds to persuade the community of Yeshua's disciples to remain steadfast in their faith. Although the community suffered many disappointments while waiting for the final redemption, they could be confident that Yeshua is the Messiah and that their allegiance to him will pay off in the end. God has taken two oaths to that effect: two unchangeable things.

First, God has taken an oath promising that he will bless Abraham's offspring and multiply them like the stars of heaven. Ultimately, all nations will be blessed through Abraham's offspring. Second, God has taken an oath that the Messiah will be inducted into an eternal priesthood called "the order of Melchizedek."

The promise to bless Abraham and to multiply his offspring like the stars refers to the flourishing of Israel in the final redemption, the nation's possession of the land, and the arrival of all the associated blessings the prophets predicted for the Messianic Era. The promise to induct the Messiah into an eternal priesthood is the subject matter of the ensuing four chapters (Hebrews 7–10). The promise refers to Yeshua's atoning role as a mediator between God and man, which grants access to the resurrection and the World to Come.

Human beings might break their oaths, but "it is impossible for God to lie." He must keep the oaths he has made. Therefore, these two certain and "unchangeable things" work together to offer a refuge of hope for all Israel and especially for the disciples who depend on the Messiah to rescue them from the coming wrath of God's judgment at the end of the age. If the disciples in the Yeshua community hoped to escape that coming wrath and enter the kingdom and the World to Come, they needed to "hold fast to the hope set before us."

> *We have this as a sure and steadfast anchor of the soul, a hope that enters into the inner place behind the curtain, where [Yeshua] has gone as a forerunner on our behalf, having become a high priest forever after the order of Melchizedek.* (HEBREWS 6:19-20)

The two unchangeable things provide the disciple with solid confidence in the future redemption through the agency of Yeshua. Confidence in the promises of God creates "a sure and steadfast anchor of the soul," which keeps the disciple from losing hope in the coming of the Messiah, the kingdom, and the World to Come.

Changing circumstances might feel as tumultuous and inconstant as the pitching of the sea in a storm, but the steadfast disciple will not be blown away by the wind or swept off by the waves. The disciple who holds fast to hope in God's promises will be rewarded in the resurrection. By means of the resurrection of the dead, that hope will usher the faithful disciple into the World to Come and the presence of God. How can we be certain? Because Yeshua of Nazareth has already entered ahead of us. Through his resurrection and ascension, he has already entered the presence of God in the resurrected physical state (not as a disembodied spirit), and there he remains, seated at the right hand of glory. He went as a forerunner of many more to follow.

Yeshua's physical entrance into the presence of God can be compared to the entrance of the high priest into the holy of holies. In his undying and incorruptible state, Yeshua has become "a high priest forever," thereby fulfilling the unchangeable oath God made to the Messiah, "You are a priest forever after the order of Melchizedek" (Psalm 110:4). Ultimately, this priest will lead Abraham's sons to glory (Hebrews 2:10) where they "shall shine like the brightness of the sky above ... like the stars forever and ever" (Daniel 12:3).

CHAPTER SIXTEEN:
MELCHIZEDEK
(HEBREWS 7:1–17)

> Based on the criteria of a resurrected and indestructible life, the Messiah has entered the priesthood of Melchizedek.

Yeshua serves as a heavenly high priest in the order of Melchizedek. The exhorter has already stated his central premise about the resurrected Messiah entering the priestly order of Melchizedek to become the source of eternal life, but he has done so only cryptically without working out the details. He introduced the idea in Hebrews 5 while discussing the suffering, death, and resurrection of the Messiah with reference to Psalm 110. The same God who (in Psalm 2) declared the Messiah to be his Son, saying, "You are my Son, today I have begotten you," also declared (in Psalm 110), "You are a priest forever, after the order of Melchizedek" (Hebrews 5:5-6). Yeshua merited to enter that high priesthood by virtue of his suffering and resurrection into the "perfect" immortal state:

> Although he was a son, he learned obedience through what he suffered. And being made perfect, he became the source of eternal salvation to all who obey him, being designated by God a high priest after the order of Melchizedek. (Hebrews 5:8-10)

The exhorter had more to say on the subject. In chapter five, he expressed some frustration and uncertainty about whether his readers possessed the spiritual maturity and biblical literacy necessary to understand the subject. He complained, "About this we have much to say, and it is hard to explain, since you have become dull of hearing" (Hebrews 5:11). He referred to the subject matter as "solid food" and contrasted it against the basic message of the gospel, which he characterized as "milk, not solid food" (Hebrews 5:12). In Hebrews 7, the exhorter returns to the subject and feeds his readers the solid food. He takes us into his argument to prove his premise about Yeshua's entrance into that mysterious priesthood.

> *For this Melchizedek, king of Salem, priest of the Most High God, met Abraham returning from the slaughter of the kings and blessed him.* (HEBREWS 7:1)

The Torah does not reveal much about Melchizedek. Three short verses in Genesis (14:18-20) tell us that Melchizedek was a king; he ministered as a priest of God, ruled a city called Salem, worshiped God Most High, blessed Abraham, and received tribute from him. The Torah does not provide any further information beyond those sparse details. As with Enoch in Genesis 5, the mysterious Melchizedek invited embellishment. Jewish and Christian traditions generously obliged.

Melchizedek was not a personal name. The name *Malchi-Tzedek* means "King of Righteousness." It seems to have functioned as an honorific enthronement title, like the name Abimelech (Father of a King) or the title Messiah (Anointed One, i.e., Christ). The title "messiah" (anointed one) applied to every king of Israel because the kings of Israel received anointing as a symbol of their investiture into the office of monarch. Likewise, it's possible that every king of Salem bore the title Melchizedek. We do not know the personal name of the Melchizedek who met Abraham in Genesis 14.

The title "King of Righteousness" readily lends itself to messianic associations. Just as Yeshua rightly wears the title of Messiah, one might also assign him the title King of Righteousness. The Prophet Jeremiah suggests as much:

> Behold, the days are coming ... when I will raise up for David a righteous Branch; and he shall reign as king and deal wisely, and shall execute justice and righteousness in the land. (Jeremiah 23:5)

> *And to him Abraham apportioned a tenth part of everything. He is first, by translation of his name, king of righteousness, and then he is also king of Salem, that is, king of peace.* (HEBREWS 7:2)

Notice how the Torah's description of this otherwise obscure Canaanite king overlaps with messianic expectations. Melchizedek ruled as king over the Canaanite city of Salem. The Bible identifies Salem as the ancient name for Jerusalem. Psalm 76:3(2) equates Salem with Zion (i.e., Jerusalem), saying, "His tabernacle is in Salem; His dwelling place also is in Zion" (NASB). The association with Jerusalem heightens the messianic imagery. The idea of a "king of righteousness" ruling over Jerusalem points toward the Messianic Era. When Messiah comes, Jerusalem will be the capital city of the kingdom of heaven on earth, and the Messiah will reign in righteousness. Furthermore, the exhorter points out that the term "King of Salem" could be read as "King of Peace" (Hebrews 7:2). Jewish eschatology waits for the righteous Messiah son of David to take up his father's throne in Jerusalem and inaugurate an era of universal peace as the "Prince of Peace."

Melchizedek came out from Jerusalem and set a table of "bread and wine" before Abraham and his men. In the coming kingdom, the Messiah will set a table for Abraham and his children, as Yeshua said, "Many will come from east and west and recline at table with Abraham, Isaac, and Jacob in the kingdom of heaven" (Matthew 8:11). Melchizedek, the king of righteousness, the king of Jerusalem, and the king of peace, gave Abraham a foretaste of the great banquet of the Messianic Era.

The Torah also identifies Melchizedek as a priest of God Most High. Functioning in that dual role of king and priest, he blessed Abraham, and he blessed God. Who was this mighty priest-king, bestowing blessing on Abraham and receiving tribute from him?

> *He is without father or mother or genealogy, having neither beginning of days nor end of life, but resembling the Son of God he continues a priest forever.* (HEBREWS 7:3)

Melchizedek appears in the Torah "without father, without mother, without genealogy, having neither beginning of days nor end of life," which is simply to say that the Torah provides none of those details for Melchizedek.

The sages had their own ideas about Melchizedek's identity. His puzzling appearance in the Torah, without any genealogical information or further explanation, inspired speculation. They speculated that he must have been Shem, the son of Noah. The chronologies in the genealogies of Genesis 11 indicate that Shem remained alive during the days of Abraham, so why not? That would mean that Melchizedek was Abraham's great, great, great grandfather, ten generations removed. Imagine meeting your grandfather from ten generations earlier!

The book of Hebrews more-or-less contradicts that traditional explanation. The exhorter insists that no one knows Melchizedek's ancestry. He uses the absence of Melchizedek's ancestry to justify Yeshua's entrance into a messianic priesthood "in the order of Melchizedek."

Not just anyone can serve as a priest in the Temple of God. The Torah limits the Levitical priesthood to the sons of Aaron. The priesthood belongs to Aaron and his sons in perpetuity:

> The priesthood shall be theirs by a statute forever. Thus you shall ordain Aaron and his sons. (Exodus 29:9)

The words "a statute forever" describe a commandment that will never be revoked "until heaven and earth pass away" (Matthew 5:18). Consequently, the priesthood belongs to the house of Aaron from generation to generation. In the Second Temple Era, priests who wanted to serve in the Sanctuary needed to provide genealogical evidence proving their Aaronic pedigree (Ezra 2:62-63). Even into our day, the descendants of Aaron know who they are. Stringent legal rulings pertaining to priestly families have preserved the genealogical lines. According to Jewish law, priests may not marry proselytes. Additional prohibitions and prerogatives unique to the priesthood have preserved family identity from generation to generation. The right to serve as a priest belongs exclusively to the descendants of Aaron. So how can Yeshua be considered a priest? He is a son of David from the tribe of Judah, not a Levite or a son of Aaron.

The exhorter points out that, according to the Torah, Melchizedek was also a priest of God Most High, yet he "does not have his descent from" the sons of Aaron. This indicates that the Torah makes room for a different kind of priesthood, namely, "the order of Melchizedek." Unlike the priestly order of Aaron, participation in the order of Melchizedek cannot be based on family ancestry because the Torah provides no genealogical information for Melchizedek. If so, by what criteria could one qualify for the priestly order of Melchizedek? The exhorter deduces a new criterion for serving in Melchizedek's priesthood from the words "a priest forever" in Psalm 110. He infers that anyone serving in the Melchizedekian priesthood must do so forever. Therefore, to qualify for the position, the candidate must be immortal. The exhorter takes note that the Torah never mentions Melchizedek's death:

> He is without father or mother or genealogy, having neither beginning of days nor end of life, but resembling the Son of God he continues a priest forever. (Hebrews 7:3)

Does this imply that Melchizedek ascended into the heavens like Enoch? Other first-century Jews had similar ideas about Melchizedek. In the Dead Sea Scrolls "the Prince of Light ... appointed from ancient times" does battle with "Belial ... [and] all the spirits of his company" (*War Rule* 1QM 13.10–12). This Prince of Light sounds remarkably like a divine Melchizedek-man in the *Melchizedek* fragment: "Melchizedek will avenge the vengeance of the judgments of God ... against Belial and all the spirits of his company" (Fragment 11QMelch/11Q13 2.13). In the scroll fragment, the Messiah-like Melchizedek proclaims the ultimate Jubilee, atones for the Sons of Light, and ushers in the final redemption. Philo, a first-century Alexandrian Jewish philosopher, understood Melchizedek in cosmic terms. He equated Melchizedek with the divine *Logos* (Word).

On the other hand, if the exhorter intends to imply that Melchizedek obtained immortality, ascended, and remains an eternal priest in the presence of God, he negates his own argument about Yeshua entering into that position by virtue of his unique attainments and exalted status. It seems more in keeping with the discussion to understand that the exhorter only intends to exploit the Torah's silence on the death of Melchizedek to make a rhetorical point. Melchizedek can be said to be "resembling the Son of God" in that the Torah does not mention his death, and as such, "he continues a priest forever" in the Torah's narrative. It's an argument from silence intended to characterize the type of priesthood that Yeshua enters. The Torah's silence on Melchizedek's ancestry and death makes him a fitting archetype for Yeshua. The statement isn't intended to imply anything more than that about the literal Melchizedek.

Was Melchizedek Yeshua?

With such lofty, mystical associations, it is easy to see why many readers have concluded that Melchizedek was a pre-incarnate appearance of Jesus in the Old Testament. However, there are some problems with this idea. If the exhorter was trying to prove that Yeshua is Melchizedek, he would not have presented his argument for Yeshua entering the "order of Melchizedek." If Yeshua is Melchizedek, why did he have to suffer and rise from the dead to enter into his own priestly order?

Notice that the Torah states that Melchizedek really was the king of the city of Salem. This implies a real government over that Jebusite city. Did the Messiah serve a term as a Canaanite king, ruling over the Jebusites for a generation or so sometime in the distant past? The face-value, literal reading of the Torah does not actually indicate that Melchizedek was anything more than a normal human being. Neither does the exhorter mean to imply that Melchizedek is Messiah or that Messiah is Melchizedek. Instead, he carefully drafts an argument that places Messiah in the priesthood of Melchizedek.

Regarding Melchizedek's supposed immortality, he says that Melchizedek was "made like the Son of God" (i.e., like an angel), and therefore, "he continues a priest forever" (Hebrews 7:3). He did not say that Melchizedek "is the Son of God." The exhorter says Melchizedek had no ancestry. Messiah, on the other hand, comes from the house of David and the tribe of Judah: "For it is evident that our Lord was descended from Judah" (Hebrews 7:14).

According to the writer of the book of Hebrews, Messiah is not Melchizedek; instead, he is inducted into the already existing priestly order of Melchizedek. He is "another priest ... in the likeness of Melchizedek" (Hebrews 7:15).

In short, the Melchizedek character who met Abraham in Genesis 14 was not Jesus making a cameo appearance in the Old Testament. Nevertheless, the enigmatic Melchizedek of Genesis 14 foreshadowed the coming Messiah, the King of Righteousness, the King of Peace, and the King of Jerusalem.

> *See how great this man was to whom Abraham the patriarch gave a tenth of the spoils! ... But this man who does not have his descent from them received tithes from Abraham.* (HEBREWS 7:4-6)

The exhorter argues that the Melchizedekian priesthood, whatever it might be, occupies a higher station than the Aaronic priesthood. Follow the simple logic. The Torah requires the Jewish people to pay tithes to the Levites, and the Levites must pay a "tithe of the tithe" to the sons of Aaron, the priests (Numbers 18:24-26). The Levites and priests who receive the tithes and the rest of the Jewish people who must pay the tithes are all children of Abraham. Yet Abraham, who occupies a station of honor higher than that of his descendants, gave a tithe to Melchizedek. This implies that Melchizedek, whoever he was, occupied a station of greater honor than that of the Levites and the Aaronic priesthood.

> *And [Melchizedek] blessed him who had the promises. It is beyond dispute that the inferior is blessed by the superior.* (HEBREWS 7:6-7)

The exhorter interrupts his argument regarding the tithe with an additional argument to prove that Melchizedek occupied a higher spiritual station than Abraham and that, consequently, the priesthood of Melchizedek occupies a higher station than that of the Levitical priesthood. The exhorter points out that if Abraham had been superior to Melchizedek, protocol would have demanded that Abraham confer the blessing upon Melchizedek rather than receiving a blessing from his inferior. This social norm might not be self-evident to us today, but it was "beyond dispute" in the Apostolic Era. The fact that Melchizedek blessed Abraham indicates that Abraham and his descendants—including the Levites and the Aaronic priesthood—occupy a lower spiritual station than that of Melchizedek.

> *One might even say that Levi himself, who receives tithes, paid tithes through Abraham, for he was still in the loins of his ancestor when Melchizedek met him.* (HEBREWS 7:9-10)

A father occupies a higher station of respect than his children. Abraham occupies a higher station than his great-grandson Levi, the progenitor of the Levites and the Aaronic priesthood. At the time of his encounter with Melchizedek, the entire Levitical tribe remained "in the loins of Abraham," so to speak. If Abraham, the grandfather of Levi and the Aaronic priesthood, paid tithes to Melchizedek, we can conclude that Melchizedek occupies a station higher than that of Aaron and the Levitical priesthood.

> *Now if perfection had been attainable through the Levitical priesthood (for under it the people received the law), what further need would there have been for another priest to arise after the order of Melchizedek, rather than one named after the order of Aaron?* (HEBREWS 7:11)

What does it mean that "the people received the law" through the Levitical priesthood? Moses made the Levitical priesthood custodians of the Torah. They were also responsible for interpreting it and transmitting it to future generations (Deuteronomy 17:9-11, 17:18, 31:9; Malachi 2:7). Nevertheless, that doesn't seem to be the point the exhorter intends to make in Hebrews 7:11. Instead, it seems to me that the exhorter has in view the divine rites and ministrations performed by Moses and the priesthood at Mount Sinai (Hebrews 9:18-22). By means of those atoning ceremonies and sacrifices, the revelation of the Torah came to the people of Israel through the agency of the Levitical priesthood.

In a previous chapter (see comments on Hebrews 2:10), we saw how the apostles refer to the unchanging state of permanence enjoyed by the resurrected in the World to Come as "the perfect." To enter "the perfect" is to enter the resurrected state and the World to Come. Employing the same language, the exhorter observes, "The Torah made nothing perfect" (Hebrews 7:19). If the Levitical priesthood were capable of ushering people into the resurrected state of the World to Come through the ceremonies and sacrifices prescribed in the Torah, there would have been no reason for God to install the Messiah into the higher priestly order of Melchizedek. The exhorter argues that there would be no need for another priestly order at all.

For when there is a change in the priesthood, there is necessarily a change in the law as well. (HEBREWS 7:12)

The installation of a new priesthood necessitates "a change in the law as well." The Messiah cannot obtain his priestly position under the authority of the Torah because the Torah sanctions only the sons of Aaron to serve as priests. Criteria for entering the priesthood of Melchizedek must be sought outside of the Torah, and that is the "change in the law" the exhorter has in mind. In an essay titled "Hebrews and the Jewish Law" (*So Great a Salvation: A Dialogue on the Atonement in Hebrews*, T&T Clark, 2021), New Testament scholar Matthew Theissen points out that the Greek noun *metathesis*, which we see translated into English as a "change" in both the priesthood and the law, is the same word that the exhorter uses to describe the ascension of Enoch:

> By faith Enoch was taken up (*metatithemi*) so that he should not see death, and he was not found, because God had taken (*metatithemi*) him. Now before he was taken (*metathesis*) he was commended as having pleased God. (Hebrews 11:5)

The same word appears in the Septuagint Greek version of Genesis 5:24 to describe the ascension of Enoch, who, according to the interpretation of first-century Jewish apocalypticism, physically ascended and entered alive into heaven. In these Enochian contexts the word *metathesis* implies a change in location (from earth to the heavens), not a legal alteration or change of substance. Naturally, the exhorter has in view the physical ascension of Enoch as he considers the theological implications of the ascension of Yeshua. He observes that, in keeping with an ascension from the earthly venue to the heavenly one, there should also be a heavenly version of the law governing the priesthood. So long as we are speaking about a heavenly ascended priest, we should also seek a heavenly ascended version of the criteria for that priesthood and not the earthbound version. (See the discussion on Hebrews 7:16 below and further discussion in the next chapter.)

According to the apocalyptic version of the story, Enoch did not die. He physically ascended to heaven, entered the angelic realm, and took on an angelic role and function. The exhorter attaches a similar elevation of the priestly functions to Yeshua as a consequence of his ascension. The exhorter elevates the laws, ceremonies, purifications, and atoning rituals of the Levitical priesthood on earth into the heavenly sphere through a *metathesis* similar to that of Enoch. It's not a change from a physical state to a spiritual state, but as in the story of Enoch, a physical elevation from the earthly to the heavenly. Much less should it be understood as an arbitrary change in divine legislation.

Replacement theology derives a serious misconception from its failure to properly understand Hebrews 7:11–12. In replacement theology, these verses are brought to prove that the priesthood of Jesus obviates the Aaronic priesthood, cancels the sacrifices, and changes the Torah. We'll correct that misinterpretation in later chapters when the exhorter offers his own solution to the tension between the two priesthoods. For now, it is sufficient to observe that since the Messiah belongs to a different priesthood from that of Aaron, his priesthood does not cancel, abolish, obviate, or replace the Aaronic priesthood. The exhorter will explain that instead of competing with the Aaronic priesthood, the Messiah conducts his priestly office in a different venue, namely, the heavenly Temple.

> *For the one of whom these things are spoken belonged to another tribe, from which no one has ever served at the altar. For it is evident that our Lord was descended from Judah, and in connection with that tribe Moses said nothing about priests.* (HEBREWS 7:13–14)

The "one of whom these things are spoken" is the Messiah. To the Messiah son of David, the LORD declared, "You are a priest forever according to the order of Melchizedek." By definition, the Messiah son of David belongs to the tribe of Judah. If Yeshua is not a direct descendant of King David and the tribe of Judah, he does not qualify to be the Messiah King. The genealogies of Yeshua in Matthew and Luke both attempt to establish Yeshua's Davidic paternity.

The Messiah belongs to the tribe of Judah and the household of David, but according to the Torah, the Levitical priests must belong to the tribe of Levi and the household of Aaron. Therefore, the criteria to qualify as Messiah and the criteria to qualify as a priest seem to be mutually exclusive.

> *This becomes even more evident when another priest arises in the likeness of Melchizedek, who has become a priest, not on the basis of a legal requirement concerning bodily descent, but by the power of an indestructible life.* (HEBREWS 7:15-16)

The exhorter has already argued that, unlike entrance into the Aaronic priesthood, entrance into the Melchizedekian priesthood is not predicated on ancestry. If it were, the Torah would have provided Melchizedek's ancestry. Instead, the exhorter finds a different criterion for entrance into the order of Melchizedek—"an indestructible life":

A candidate for the priesthood of Melchizedek must be "a priest forever." This is the "*metathesis* of the law" mentioned in Hebrews 7:12. The higher heavenly criteria that qualifies a candidate for the heavenly priesthood is not Aaronic ancestry but immortality. The exhorter derives this metathetical criterion from Psalm 110, which describes the Messiah as "a priest forever":

> For it is witnessed of Him, "You are a priest forever after the order of Melchizedek." (Hebrews 7:17)

Mortal men need not apply for the position. The exhorter concludes that the Messiah entered the order of Melchizedek based not on his ancestry but on the criteria of his indestructible life—something he obtained through his resurrection from the dead. The rest of Hebrews 7 further explores the implications of that new criterion for priesthood.

King and Priest

The Epistle to the Hebrews makes no mention of the messianic prophecy in Zechariah 6:11-13, but that prophecy undergirds the discussion about the Messiah's dual role as king and priest. The prophecy casts the Messiah in both roles. Zechariah uttered the prophecy not long after the exiles had returned to Jerusalem from captivity in Babylon.

In those days, the city and the Temple lay in ruins. Messianic expectations ran high. The people looked for Messiah to return the rest of the exiles, reestablish David's throne in Jerusalem, and rebuild the Temple. But where was he?

In those days, a man named Yehoshua (Joshua) served as high priest. The Jewish people returning from Babylon no longer spoke Hebrew as their first language. After seventy years in the Babylonian exile, they spoke Aramaic, so they referred to the high priest Yehoshua by the Aramaic form of his name: Yeshua. The LORD told the Prophet Zechariah to make a kingly crown and set it on the head of Yeshua, the high priest. He was then told to declare a prophecy over him: "Behold, the man whose name is the Branch," who will "be a priest on his throne." The prophecy seems to indicate that the man "whose name is the Branch" reconciles and combines the offices of priest and king:

> Take from them silver and gold, and make a crown, and set it on the head of [Yeshua], the son of Jehozadak, the high priest. And say to him, "Thus says the LORD of hosts, 'Behold, the man whose name is the Branch: for he shall branch out from his place, and he shall build the temple of the LORD. It is he who shall build the temple of the LORD and shall bear royal honor, and shall sit and rule on his throne. And there shall be a priest on his throne, and the counsel of peace shall be between them both.'" (Zechariah 6:11-13)

"Branch" is a title for the Messiah derived from the earlier prophets Isaiah (4:2, 11:1) and Jeremiah (23:5). Zechariah predicts that Branch will be a man named Yeshua who will serve as both king and priest. How can these two offices be reconciled if priests must be sons of Aaron from the tribe of Levi and kings must be sons of David from the tribe of Judah? According to the rules of tribal identity and Jewish genealogy, a person cannot be a son of Aaron and a son of David, even if he had ancestors from both lines. The exhorter offers us a bold solution by suggesting that the Messiah serves in a different priesthood, that of Melchizedek, a man who served as both king and priest.

This was good news for the Jewish believers in the first century who had been forced out of the Temple and cut off from the priesthood. It is still good news today—good news for Israel, for the exiles, and for all the Jewish people who have lived without a Temple and a functioning priesthood for nearly two thousand years. It is good news for everyone who seeks to draw near to God because without a priest, you cannot draw near to the living God. It is good news for sinners like us who have no priest to carry out a sacrifice or apply atoning blood to the altar on our behalf.

CHAPTER SEVENTEEN:
THE OATH AND THE LAW
(HEBREWS 7:18–28)

> The heavenly priesthood of the Messiah is efficacious for attaining eternal life without replacing the office or function of the Levitical priesthood.

The Epistle to the Hebrews speaks of a change of the priesthood. The author of the exhortation speaks of our Master Yeshua entering into a high priesthood distinct from the Levitical priesthood instituted in the Torah. The exhorter says, "When there is a change in the priesthood, there is necessarily a change in the law as well" (Hebrews 7:12). This passage seems to revoke the Aaronic priesthood and topple the Torah in one swift stroke. "The priesthood is changed," and along with it comes "a change of Torah as well."

That interpretation forces the Scriptures to contradict themselves. The Bible declares that the Torah is eternal and unchanging. The eternal, unchanging Torah says the priesthood will belong to Aaron and his sons as an eternal statute. If God changed the Torah and revoked his promises to the house of Aaron, the exhorter could simply have written, "The sons of Aaron are no longer priests because Jesus is now the only true priest." He did not say that, nor does he mean to imply it. God will not change his own laws, nor will he break his covenant promises. The replacement-theology interpretation, which posits the replacement of the Torah with a new covenant, contradicts our Master's own teaching, "Do not think I came to abolish the Torah," and it contradicts the

Torah's own testimony—that the commandments pertaining to the priesthood, the Temple, and the sacrifices are eternal statutes.

The answer to the apparent conflict lies in the carefully structured argument of the book of Hebrews. The exhorter realizes Yeshua is not a priest in the Aaronic order of priests. He clearly states that objection and validates the ongoing role of the Aaronic priesthood:

> For it is evident that our Lord was descended from Judah, and in connection with that tribe Moses said nothing about priests. (Hebrews 7:14)

> Now if [Messiah] were on earth, he would not be a priest at all, since there are priests who offer the gifts according to the [Torah] [i.e., the sons of Aaron]. (Hebrews 8:4)

According to the book of Hebrews, the Aaronic priesthood retains its legitimate office. The Messiah does not supplant the sons of Aaron or their right to the priesthood. The exhorter says that if the risen Messiah remained on earth, he would not function as a priest because he was born from the tribe of Judah and not from the house of Aaron. The priesthood belongs to the sons of Aaron by an eternal statute.

> *For on the one hand, a former commandment is set aside because of its weakness and uselessness (for the law made nothing perfect); but on the other hand, a better hope is introduced, through which we draw near to God.* (HEBREWS 7:18-19)

Which "former commandment" does the exhorter have in view? Why does he characterize that commandment as weak and useless? Remember, his argument hinges not on a contrast between Judaism and Christianity but rather on the dichotomy between the Levitical priesthood and the priesthood of Melchizedek.

If so, the "former commandment" refers to the Torah's rule about the priesthood belonging exclusively to the sons of Aaron:

> The priesthood shall be theirs by a statute forever. Thus you shall ordain Aaron and his sons. (Exodus 29:9)

That rule grants the Levitical priesthood to the sons of Aaron. It cannot be canceled; it remains valid to this day and until heaven and earth pass away. The exhorter does not suggest that the "former commandment" has been canceled; instead, that statute has been "set aside" as a criterion for entrance into the order of Melchizedek because "when there is a change in the priesthood, there is necessarily a change in the law as well" (Hebrews 7:12). As explained in the previous chapter, it's not a "change" in the Torah's rules but a metathesis, a transfer of the rule to a heavenly context. A different rule governs the criteria for entering the order of Melchizedek. Qualification for that priesthood is not based on Levitical ancestry but rather upon the criteria spelled out in Psalm 110: an indestructible and immortal life.

When read out of context and through the lens of traditional theology, Hebrews 7:18-19 sounds as if the writer of Hebrews calls the Torah "weak and useless." On the contrary, he refers to the criteria governing qualification for the earthly priesthood as "weak and useless" for procuring "the perfect," i.e., the resurrection and a share in the World to Come:

> For the [Torah] appoints men in their weakness as high priest, but the word of the oath [i.e., Psalm 110], which came later than the [Torah], appoints a Son who has been made perfect forever. (Hebrews 7:28)

The Aaronic priesthood is insufficient for the task of attaining forgiveness for sins and eternal life because the priests themselves are merely mortal men, guilty of their own sins and doomed to die a mortal death. An Aaronic priest must offer a sacrifice first for "his own sins and then for those of the people" (Hebrews 7:27). The priesthood belongs to the house of Aaron by an irrevocable, eternal statute, but that priesthood is unable to bring "perfection." Only in that regard is it "weak and useless."

What Has Been Set Aside?

Replacement theology has misconstrued almost the entire argument. It is widely supposed that the book of Hebrews delegitimizes the Temple, the priesthood, and the Torah all at once by abolishing the Aaronic priesthood and replacing it with the priesthood of Yeshua.

On the contrary, the exhorter goes to some length to demonstrate that this is not the case. He wants his readers to understand that the priesthood in which Yeshua serves is not the same order of priests as the one occupied by the sons of Aaron. Indeed, by virtue of being a son of David, Yeshua does not qualify for service in that priesthood.

The LORD "set aside" the former commandment that spoke about the eternal statute guaranteeing the Aaronic priesthood when he swore to the Messiah, "You are a priest forever after the order of Melchizedek" (Psalm 110:4). In this argument, the exhorter contrasts two eternal statutes and two priesthoods:

> Aaron and his sons ... the priesthood shall be theirs by a statute forever. (Exodus 29:9)

> The LORD has sworn and will not change his mind, "You are a priest forever after the order of Melchizedek." (Psalm 110:4)

One passage says that the priesthood belongs to Aaron and his sons forever; the other passage says that the Messiah will be a priest forever. The exhorter resolves the contradiction by observing that the two passages speak about two different orders of priesthood. The Messiah attained his priesthood in the order of Melchizedek "not on the basis of a legal requirement concerning bodily descent [i.e., Aaronic ancestry], but by the power of an indestructible life. For it is witnessed of him, 'You are a priest forever after the order of Melchizedek'" (Hebrews 7:16-17). Only an undying immortal can meet the qualification of being a "priest forever." Yeshua meets that qualification because he has conquered mortal death.

Were it possible to cancel the eternal statute of Exodus 29:9 and replace the Aaronic priesthood, the exhorter's entire discussion about Melchizedek and his priestly order would be superfluous.

Weak and Useless

As a tool for attaining the resurrection of the dead, the Levitical worship system could be only "weak and useless." The Aaronic priesthood did not have the authority to justify sinners or secure their entrance to the World to Come. That was not the priesthood's job. The purpose of the priesthood was to facilitate the worship of God in the holy Sanctuary here on earth and maintain the covenant between God and Israel.

They performed covenant maintenance by conducting the sacrificial services, applying the blood of sacrifices to the altar, and entering the presence of God to intercede and atone for the nation. Their efforts preserved the covenant relationship and bestowed God's blessing upon the nation. It was not a priest's job to qualify worshipers for the resurrection of the dead. Paul expresses a similar thought in Romans 8:

> God has done what the [Torah], weakened by the flesh, could not do. By sending his own Son in the likeness of sinful flesh and for sin, he condemned sin in the flesh, in order that the righteous requirement of the [Torah] might be fulfilled in us, who walk not according to the flesh but according to the Spirit. (Romans 8:3-4)

What is it that the Torah cannot do? Paul has in view justification, salvation, the resurrection, the kingdom, and the World to Come. The Torah cannot accomplish those things, and in that regard, the Torah is weak. The Torah is not deficient in any sense; rather, it is "weakened by the flesh." The weakness of the Torah is the weakness of human beings who fail to meet the Torah's righteous standards. The Torah defines righteousness and sin. It provides God's righteous standard, his code of wrong and right, and his eternal law. It fails to obtain the resurrection of the dead only because "all have sinned and fall short of the glory of God" and "the wages of sin is death" (Romans 3:23, 6:23). Yeshua of Nazareth accomplishes the things the Torah cannot do. Having conquered death and risen to eternal life, he is not "weakened by the flesh." Through the merit of his righteousness and the favor his suffering earned in the sight of God, his disciples are granted the privilege of drawing near to God and entering into the resurrected state of "the perfect."

> *And it was not without an oath. For those who formerly became priests were made such without an oath, but this one was made a priest with an oath by the one who said to him: "The Lord has sworn and will not change his mind, 'You are a priest forever.'"* (HEBREWS 7:20-21)

The English Standard Version betrays its theological bias by interjecting the word "formerly" into Hebrews 7:21: "For those who *formerly* became priests were made such without an oath." That translation makes it sound as if the Aaronic priesthood is defunct. The New American Standard succinctly renders the statement without the bias, "For they indeed became priests without an oath."

When the LORD ordained Aaron and his sons into the priesthood, he granted them exclusive rights to the office as an eternal statute (Exodus 29:9), but he did not swear an oath as he did concerning the Messiah in Psalm 110. This does not imply that God might retract Aaron's rights to the Levitical priesthood, but it does add an emphatic thrust to the perpetuity of the Messiah's appointment to the order of Melchizedek: "The LORD has sworn and will not change his mind, 'You are a priest forever after the order of Melchizedek'" (Psalm 110:4). As mortal men with limited lifespans, Aaron and his sons could not serve in perpetuity. The oath promises that the Messiah will be "a priest forever."

> *This makes [Yeshua] the guarantor of a better covenant.* (HEBREWS 7:22)

The Levitical priests were charged with maintaining the covenant relationship between God and Israel. Just as there are two priesthoods, there are two covenants. The Levitical priesthood stewards the covenant God made with Israel at Sinai. The messianic priesthood of the order of Melchizedek, therefore, must steward a different covenant—a better covenant. The oath in Psalm 110 "makes [Yeshua] the guarantor of a better covenant" than the one administered by the Levitical priesthood because it guarantees his eternal role. We will discuss the "better covenant" in later chapters.

> *The former priests were many in number, because they were prevented by death from continuing in office, but he holds his priesthood permanently, because he continues forever.* (HEBREWS 7:23-24)

When the English Standard Version of the Bible says, "the *former* priests," this suggests they are no longer priests, but the translators have inserted the word "former" into their translation. It does not belong there because it is not found in the Greek text underlying this passage. The Greek translates literally as "those indeed are many who have become priests." It does not say, "The former priests were many."

Notice that the English Standard Version also translates the verb into a past tense form by saying that "the former priests *were* many," implying that a new dispensation has begun and that their priestly status is no longer to be recognized or that their priesthood no longer functions. A literal translation of the Greek reads the sentence in the present tense, "Those indeed *are* many who have become priests, because by death they *are* hindered from remaining" (Young's Literal Translation, emphasis mine).

Why are there so "many who have become priests?" Because their mortal, human deaths prevent them from serving eternally in their office as priests. When they die, new generations of priests take their place. An Aaronic priest cannot meet the criteria of the order of Melchizedek: "You are a priest forever." When he dies, his priesthood ends.

> *Consequently, he is able to save to the uttermost those who draw near to God through him, since he always lives to make intercession for them.* (HEBREWS 7:25)

Because Yeshua has already entered the immortal state of the perfect through his resurrection, he is "able to save to the uttermost ... since he always lives to make intercession." The word "uttermost" refers to the extreme limit in this life and the next, from this world to the kingdom to the World to Come. Yeshua's life spans all those eras. Simply put, "Yeshua is able to save you for eternal life because, unlike normal priests, he lives eternally."

Those who seek God through him will be saved from death "since he always lives to make intercession for them." Much as the Levitical priesthood entered the presence of God on earth to make atonement in the Sanctuary on earth, the Messiah is able to make atonement in the presence of God in the heavenly Sanctuary. The prayers, blessings, and atoning intercession of the Aaronic priesthood pertain only to life in this world, but the prayers and intercession of Yeshua's high priesthood are efficacious even into the World to Come. His atoning intercession will not fail, nor will his petitions go unheeded.

Even now, to this very hour, the Master actively intercedes in the presence of God to atone for his people and pray for his disciples. If the Master is praying for us, what do we have to fear? If he is interceding for us, why are we so worried and filled with anxiety and despair? If we trust him to deliver our souls from Gehenna and raise us from the dead, should we not also trust him to deliver us from the much less consequential vexations and problems that face us today in this world? Are his prayers efficacious only for the afterlife? The exhorter says, "He always lives to make intercession for them."

It reminds me of a story from the Gospels. Once, the disciples were in a fishing boat on Lake Galilee when a strong headwind rose. The Master was not with them. They strained against the wind and the waves all night, to no avail. They did not know that the Master watched them from a hilltop overlooking the lake where he had gone to spend the night in prayer. As he prayed, he saw them straining at the oars, for the wind was against them. At length, he walked out to them, striding over the waves. The atoning intercession of our Master should give us confidence not only for the life to come but also for every trial we face in this life.

> *For it was indeed fitting that we should have such a high priest, holy, innocent, unstained, separated from sinners, and exalted above the heavens.* (HEBREWS 7:26)

Where is the venue of the Aaronic priesthood? Here on earth, in the Temple, in Jerusalem. Where is the venue of Messiah's priesthood? Not on earth, not in the Temple, but "separated from sinners, and exalted above the heavens" in the Sanctuary of heavenly Jerusalem.

In this way, Yeshua's priesthood utterly transcends the Aaronic priesthood. The men who serve in the Temple are ordinary human beings, and the priests on earth must sanctify themselves to serve in the holy place, but Yeshua is sanctified by resurrection. The priests on earth must do their best to live godly lives worthy of their office, but Yeshua is innocent, meaning he committed no sins and carries no guilt. The priests on earth can be disqualified from their duties by all types of Levitical defilements, but the resurrected Messiah is unstained—neither spiritual nor Levitical defilement can cling to him or disqualify him from his priestly service. The priests on earth offer sin offerings on behalf of others, but they, too, commit sins like all human beings. Yeshua is sinless and, therefore, separated from sinners. Having entered the immortal and perfect state, he can neither commit a sin nor be sullied by the sins of others. The priests on earth conduct their priestly rites only on earth, but Yeshua conducts his priesthood "exalted above the heavens."

He has no need, like those high priests, to offer sacrifices daily, first for his own sins and then for those of the people, since he did this once for all when he offered up himself. (HEBREWS 7:27)

The exhorter compares the suffering and death of Yeshua to the sacrifices offered by the Levitical priesthood. He depicts Yeshua as a priest offering himself as a sacrifice on behalf of Israel: "He offered up himself." Unlike the priesthood on earth, Yeshua's priesthood offers only one sacrifice, and that only once.

On Yom Kippur, the high priest first offered a bull as a sin offering for himself and his household, then offered sin offerings on behalf of the nation (Leviticus 16). That order of priority established the protocol for the daily services in the Temple. The priests needed first to amend their own shortcomings before they could assist others. Yeshua has no need to offer sacrifices on his own behalf because he has committed no sins or transgressions.

For the law appoints men in their weakness as high priests, but the word of the oath, which came later than the law, appoints a Son who has been made perfect forever. (HEBREWS 7:28)

The Torah appoints men in their weakness into the office of high priest. As mortals, they cannot offer immortality to others while they themselves remain under the dominion of death. As sinners, they cannot offer expiation of sin when they themselves are slaves to sin. The exhorter spoke earlier about this weakness when saying, "A former commandment is set aside because of its weakness and uselessness" (Hebrews 7:18).

The oath to the Messiah in Psalm 110 "came later than the Torah," indicating that it does not have the Levitical priesthood or the Torah's criteria for priesthood in view. Instead, it "appoints a Son [cf. Psalm 2:7] who has been made perfect forever." That is to say, he has entered into the immortal and incorruptible state of the resurrected.

This does not mean that the Levitical priesthood is out of business. They still have their job, role, and place in the worship of God: custodianship over God's holy Sanctuary on earth and the maintenance of God's covenant with Israel. The prophets predict that the Aaronic priesthood will be restored to that role and function in the Messianic Era yet to come (e.g., Jeremiah 33:20–28; Ezekiel 44).

The two priesthoods are not in competition. In the days of the apostles, many priests became disciples of Yeshua: "The number of the disciples multiplied greatly in Jerusalem, and a great many of the priests became obedient to the faith" (Acts 6:7). Those priests saw no conflict between their priestly roles in the Temple and the role of Yeshua as a priest in the order of Melchizedek. They did not resign their positions in the priesthood on account of their newfound faith in the Messiah.

The writer of the book of Hebrews originally offered his word of exhortation to console the brothers and sisters who had lost access to the Temple and the ministry of the Levitical priesthood. The message also consoles us who live today without a Temple and a priesthood. We have a high priest in heaven who bestows his blessing on us, intercedes, atones, and prays for us. He said, "Behold, I am with you always, even to the end of the age."

www.ingramcontent.com/pod-product-compliance
Lightning Source LLC
Chambersburg PA
CBHW070136080526
44586CB00015B/1711